The Safety Net

Practical suggestions for updating education, aggressively fostering small business development, and combating poverty and homelessness.

By Coral Scribner

Wild Raccoon Press .com

Wild Raccoon Press

First Edition

Published by Wild Raccoon Press

WildRaccoonPress.com

Copyright © 2012 by Coral Scribner

ISBN: 978-1-300-03825-2

Wild Raccoon Press .com

Table of Contents

Detailed Table of Contents

About This Book

Ask Questions, Debate Answers

Everything in this book comes from my own experiences. I am not a politician, lawyer, accountant, case worker, manager of a non-profit or other professional with recognized training and knowledge in these topics. I am a person who has dealt with poverty directly and often wished I had access to the benefits provided by many of programs described.

Since these ideas seem to be uniquely different from those currently being discussed on the national level, I am providing them as a starting point for discussions among people who are either currently in poverty or actively involved in working to address the needs of poor people everywhere. Therefore, my suggestion is to read this book, gather together a group of family and friends, and have a good time debating the ideas presented.

Safety Nets, Communism and Socialism

There are people who will read this book and start screaming words like communism and socialism. I am not a political scientist but I strongly suspect the primary difference between what I am proposing and those particular objections can be summed up in a single word: choice. While I have included provisions allowing the courts to mandate participation under certain circumstances, this is otherwise an entirely voluntary series of suggestions.

Also, I would direct you to the last chapter, which discusses the ways in which the American lifestyle needs to change. Safety nets are both good and necessary, but every individual is responsible for using these resources to develop a lifestyle based on strong networks of small family businesses and increased freedom from government reliance.

Safety nets are there to catch you when you fall, but the programs described in this book are designed to provide the opportunity to become fully self-sustaining to those who are both willing and able to help themselves.

Guaranteed Minimum Income (GMI) or Citizens' Income

The Guaranteed Work Program (GWP) described in chapter one contains similarities to the Basic Income Guarantee or Citizens Income first proposed in 1795 by American revolutionary Thomas Paine. Our current system of legally requiring employers to pay a minimum wage is a variation on the theory of a Citizens Income.

The primary difference between the Citizens Income and this proposed Guaranteed Work Program is the option to choose between participation and refraining from participation. While businesses, non-profits and farms of all sizes are required to adhere to both federal and state minimum wage laws, they are not legally required to offer jobs through the GWP or take advantage of the benefits provided. Individuals are also free to choose to utilize the services offered or find another source of income. The only exceptions to this rule occur when an individual is court-ordered to participate in order to resolve specific legal issues, or when an existing employee chooses to participate in the program, thereby involving the employer.

Bailing Out the Victims

IN 2008 and 2009 hundreds of banks received enormous government bailouts and then continued to aggressively pursue recovering debts from customers, many of whom were the victims of predatory lending practices. Families facing foreclosure and individuals forced into bankruptcy were, justifiably, angry. If you've been looking for a way to force banks and other financial institutions to bail out their customers, then please read the suggestions outlined in this book!

Safety Nets and the Future

Most of this book details ideas for programs, policies and resources that address the immediate needs of people in poverty. Many of these suggestions include features geared toward fostering small business development, improving public education, and providing opportunities for attending college without incurring debt – all of which help to reduce the number of people living in poverty.

The last chapter is somewhat theoretical, but it is important that every reader understand the difference between meeting short-term needs and addressing long-term goals. A truly effective safety-net will help both individuals and communities move into financial situations that are not reliant on these services.

There will always be people in need of some form of assistance. Therefore, all welfare programs must be designed for long-term use. But a truly successful program will help communities to establish safety-nets of their own -- help people find ways to help themselves.

Grammar, Readability, Errors and Opinions

If you are the kind of person who simply cannot read anything without a red pen clutched in your hand, then allow me to enlist your assistance! As a single parent with a toddler, I wrote this book at night, early in the morning, during naptime and while my child was quietly playing by himself. Sometimes this meant I was able to get a couple of hours uninterrupted and other times it did not.

I have done my best to assure that everything was properly addressed, grammatical errors were removed, and sentences were clear and concise. However, under the circumstances, I would have preferred to hire an editor to go over the entire work and provide a list of corrections and suggestions for improvement before publication. Sadly, that expense was beyond the capabilities of my extremely minimal budget.

If you would like to put your red pen to work and participate in a little volunteer editing, please visit the contact us page at the Wild Raccoon Press website (WildRaccoonPress.com). Using the form provided, send all corrections, suggestions for readability, and other commentary to the attention of the editor.

Chapter 1: Guaranteed Work Program (GWP)

Responding to a youngster's complaints about boredom on a beautiful summer day with the phrase "I'll *find* something for you to do!" is something that parents and grandparents everywhere are apt to do. Sports enthusiasts may enjoy the following quote comes from the 2010 article "The Legend of Bubba Starling" by Dirk Chatelain of the <u>World-Herald</u> (emphasis mine):

> "Bubba dreams of eating up fly balls like Jim Edmonds. He dreams of hitting laser beams to all fields like Joe Mauer. The images come mostly from his imagination — his family won't get cable TV until he's 17. No video games, either.
>
> "If you want something to do," his father, Jim, says, "go out and find a ball. ***Or I'll find something for you to do.***"

Over many years of dealing with poverty on one level or another, I could not help but notice the sheer number of people who wanted to work but could not find viable employment despite the existence of a large amount of work needing to be done. Basic logic would suggest that people wanting work and loads of work waiting to be completed makes for a perfect match! But everywhere you look there is a consistent disconnect – arranging it and paying for it. The Guaranteed Work Program (GWP) seeks to resolve that disconnect.

What vs. How

Everything mentioned in this proposal is technologically and economically possible. However, legally speaking, it may require some new interpretations of existing laws, reformation of current financial systems, or the establishment of new laws. Sadly, I am neither a lawyer nor a politician, so I can only provide the idea, not the means by which to make it a reality.

Definition of Poverty

Poverty is defined by a lack of financial income and other resources. It is nothing more or less than a state of living resulting from a bank account total and an income flow that is numerically below the number needed to cover a middle class lifestyle.

One problem faced by many people struggling with poverty is an unrealistic official definition of the poverty line. Government agencies and non-profit organizations use calculations based on a poverty level that is consistently defined by an annual income that is set far below the amount actually needed to meet basic needs.

For the purposes of this book, I will be using 200% of a fictitious Federal minimum wage as my definition of poverty in sample calculations. This is also the basis for suggested modifications to the current bankruptcy system. It is possible that 200% of minimum wage is *too low.* Unfortunately, an accurate calculation of a true poverty line requires more data than I have available to me at the time of the writing of this book. However, the section on the true cost of living specifically addresses the data needed for an accurate calculation of both the poverty line as well as the definition of a middle class lifestyle.

One of the advantages of this program is the fact that a wide variety of individuals would be using it to cover all household expenses and basic necessities. This presents an enormous data-gathering opportunity, which can then be used to more accurately calculate the true cost of living in all areas of the country.

Poverty is Not

In addition to the mathematical calculation of a realistic poverty line in the United States I would like to provide the following short list of things that poverty is not:

- A crime
- A disease
- A form of laziness
- A lifestyle choice
- A lifestyle that 'certain people' deserve
- A mental illness
- A punishment from God
- An indication of reduced mental capacity
- Grounds for accusing or implying that an individual is an unfit parent

- Grounds for forcing or coercing a person into aborting a pregnancy
- Grounds for forcing or coercing a person into sterilization surgery
- Grounds for forcing or coercing a person to give his or her children up for adoption
- Grounds for refusing a person employment or housing
- Justification for harassment or bullying
- Proof of weakness or fallibility

Definition of Frugality

The key difference between people who choose to live frugally and people who are in poverty is simply this – choice. Individuals who choose to take a low paying job, rent an apartment in a poor area of town, and/or significantly reduce their spending for political, religious, environmental or other reasons are not living in poverty.

When a person has the resources to live a middle or upper class lifestyle, but chooses to live on significantly less, they are participating in a frugal lifestyle. This is an admirable and environmentally friendly way to live, as well as a highly educational experience for anyone who has never dealt with poverty or frugality before.

However, having the ability to choose to live differently at any time is an extremely important difference. Simply knowing that you can choose to go elsewhere, at any time, changes your own perspective on things. There is no chance of finding yourself in a situation that you simply cannot get out of, because you have accessible resources waiting to be used.

People who are truly living in poverty face far more challenges, many of which provide roadblocks to securing viable employment. For example, people from all income levels treat people living frugally significantly differently than they treat poor people, partly because of the sheer number of negative stereotypes associated with poverty. Therefore, people in poverty have fewer opportunities made available to them.

To put it plainly, the difference between people who live frugally and people in poverty is the exact same difference that lies between the following two people sitting in separate jail cells: 1) Frugality has a key in his or her pocket and can leave the cell at any time, and 2) Poverty has neither a key nor a contact outside the cell with access to a key that might be used on his or her behalf.

Introduction to the Proposed GWP

The key objective behind the Guaranteed Work Program (GWP) is to create a practical, workable and easily accessible method for people to find work, pay their debts, and even save a little money. This is not a charity or a handout, it's a job. The people participating are receiving a wage in exchange for part- or full-time work.

Simply providing limited amounts of food and cash barely gets a person through the day. Threatening people with severe consequences if they are unable to find a job or pay their debts, without providing reasonable legal options, creates a situation where the only viable option it to participate in illegal and potentially dangerous behaviors.

The current system not only encourages illegal activity, it actually openly supports it. I have known women who attempted to get onto welfare because they wanted to get out of prostitution but made the mistake of admitting to their methods of survival. These women were denied all forms of state assistance because they *already had a job*. The court system is filled with stories about people who started, or returned to, criminal activities ranging from theft to murder because they had to pay off any number of debts, they were behind on child support payments, or they already had a criminal record and were left with no other options for survival.

Simply shouting "get a job" does not make a job available. However, if a job is provided to a person, and that person does what he or she is supposed to do, then society as a whole benefits from the actions of a good citizen. Conversely, if an individual refuses to take advantage of the legal options available, or enters the program and chooses to continue pursuing illegal activities anyway, then the court system has a reason and a right to judge that person harshly.

The bottom line is this – there are many positive things that need to be done. Give people the option to do honest, positive work, knowing that all financial problems would be dealt with in a fair and reasonable manner, and there is a very strong possibility that a significant (and specific) portion of criminal activity would be eliminated.

Reliability

One of the primary advantages to the Guaranteed Work Program (GWP) is the fact that it will always be there. Unlike current government assistance programs, there are no lifetime limits for participation. An individual can utilize the GWP as often as he or she needs. Also, there are no restrictions based on criminal history, credit ratings, income level, family size or disability. Anyone who needs it, for any reason, can participate.

Full-Time Employment Deserves a Middle Class Lifestyle

The expectation that a full-time job should be enough to establish and maintain a middle class lifestyle is a reasonable one to have. It is also beneficial to society as a whole when this expectation becomes reality.

When it is not possible to make ends meet despite holding down a full-time job, it forces people to find a better paying job, a second job, work the system in an effort to secure welfare benefits, take on under-the-table work, or participate in illegal activities. All of these activities take time away from family and community, which has long-reaching negative consequences that eventually effect on society as a whole.

Conversely, when an individual or a family has a reasonably comfortable middle class lifestyle provided by a single full-time job, the effect on the surrounding community and society as a whole is positive. Also, it gives the individuals involved a nice life that is worth protecting.

The people who are most likely to commit crimes are those who believe they are above the law and those who have nothing to lose. If you spend your entire life being bailed out by parents with large amounts of money and high-powered lawyers, then there is no reason to fear the consequences of criminal action. If you spend your entire life having to fight to survive, being given few (if any) legal options for making the money necessary to put food on the table, and regularly facing accusations of being untrustworthy or an active criminal simply because of where you live, what you look like, or your income level; then, you have nothing to lose.

The people in the middle, with nice lives and moderate incomes, are the ones who are most affected by the consequences of criminal activity. These are the people who are most aware of what they have to lose.

Website and Mobile Applications Contest

It would be beneficial to human services programs of all kinds to have access to detailed numbers illustrating the true cost of living in any geographical area. To this end, it would be equally beneficial for the government to issue a website and mobile application development challenge. Simply create a website that lists the criteria for the calculations, allows people to vote on their favorites, and requests feedback from users. The winner would be provided a cash prize and a prominent button and link on the home page of every human services website in the United States.

Some example of application criteria include: 1) collecting published prices from online, national and local retail establishments, 2) identifying and presenting reasonable mid-range that consists of both a high and low number, 3) ensuring that the numbers consist entirely of standard retail prices and not discounts or sales, 4) allowing users to identify specific items for comparison purposes (e.g.: salmon, steak and cheese can have significantly different prices in different regions), and 5) provide all necessary functionality through a website and a series of mobile applications developed for use on multiple platforms.

If You Work, It Will Be Covered

Instead of simply shouting "find a job" at every applicant who walks through the door, a Guaranteed Work Program (GWP) case worker enters a client's skills, limitations and objectives into a database and it pulls up a list of available jobs. The client chooses a job off the list and, if accepted by the employer, shows up for work. As long as the employee is reliable and the job is done reasonably well, all necessities would be covered.

Expectations of Modern Workers

One of the interesting aspects about the GWP is the list of 'basics.' There would be many people who look at both the basics and benefits lists and immediately insist many of these things are unnecessary.

There will also be the invariable comparison to workers in third world countries who manage to get by without running water.

It is important to keep in mind that these lists are built out of modern-day expectations placed on workers in the United States. In this country, employees must bathe with far more regularity than workers in third world countries, or risk being fired for poor hygiene. Therefore, running water and other utilities are a necessity. There is the expectation that an employee will present the proper image by wearing a certain kind or standard or clothing, which occasionally means an individual must buy new instead of used. Cell phones, email and internet access are no longer luxuries; they are an integral part of the fabric of both private and professional life, and have become standard methods of communication. Employers no longer ask if a person has email or internet access, they simply assume everyone does. Additionally, auto insurance is (technically) legally required of every person holding a valid driver's license, regardless of whether or not he or she owns a car. Soon, health insurance will also become a legal requirement.

In short, everything required of an employee in the United States, both professionally and legally, must be taken into consideration.

True Cost of Living

The amount of money made available to each participant would be based on the true cost of living drawn from a total calculation of the standard retail cost of basic necessities in a geographical area. The GWP will gather real data from program participants, but that information must always be tempered by the possibility that all necessary supplies may have to be purchased at standard retail prices – there's no guarantee local stores would be offering sale prices.

Basics

1. Child care, schooling, and school supplies
2. Clothes
3. Communications – Phone, Internet
4. Food
5. Health insurance and health care
6. Household supplies and incidentals

7. Insurance -- home, auto, and life
8. Rent or mortgage payment
9. Transportation
10. Utilities

Benefits

1. Debt repayment
2. Entertainment fund
3. Financial education classes and services
4. Investment fund
5. Relocation allowance
6. Retirement fund
7. Vacation (1 - 2 weeks)

Assessing Immediate Needs: Home, Auto, Finances, and More

This is a potential aspect of the GWP that most participants will prefer to avoid. However, because people would be coming from a wide range of situations, experiences and backgrounds, it may be necessary to create a standardized system for inspecting an individual's existing property for the purposes of evaluating needs. A team of specialists could be created, for the purpose of evaluating and addressing all initial problems, such as:

1. **Attorney(s)** – look over total debts and determine whether or not client needs to file bankruptcy. Examine legal aspects of debts owed and/or participation in the program and ensure the participant is aware of all necessary details.
2. **Auto mechanic** -- look at the family vehicle, address any immediate needs, and/or recommend a new form of transportation.
3. **Building inspector** -- examine all aspects of the participant's home or apartment building and provide a thorough report detailing its needs for immediate and future repairs, as well as any issues regarding safety and building regulations.

4. **Clothing buyer** -- identify the necessary clothes and ensure that an individual is supplied with items that fit properly. This may involve simply taking accurate measurements of every person in the family, ordering the necessary items, and requesting alterations when necessary.
5. **Computer technician** -- assess what the family already has, identify work and school needs, secure the necessary hardware and fix or troubleshoot other issues that may arise.
6. **Early childhood development specialist** -- provide books, toys and supplies suited to children of all ages.
7. **Home organizer** -- help to assess or locate an appropriate living space, assess the immediate needs for organizing, cleaning, household and kitchen supplies. This person would also secure and arrange for the delivery of furniture, appliances, linens, etc.
8. **Tax accountant** -- look over all existing paperwork, file back and current taxes, research the credit report, identify all existing debts, and work out a payment plan that addresses everything.

Clearly, someone who is homeless needs significantly more help setting up an apartment, securing household supplies, and pulling together a wardrobe. However, people who are already living in a fully furnished house or apartment may need a very specific list of items, assistance with a vehicle, or a wardrobe that suits the job being provided through the program. Regardless of circumstance, every participant must be made aware of the potential need for a home, computer and vehicle inspection, as well as the possibility that he entire family would be scheduled for clothing size measurements.

Budgeting and Incentives

Cash-Only Lifestyle

The only financial accounts a participant would be allowed are a savings account and a checking account with a debit card – all checks would be confiscated and the bank will not issue any additional checks until the program has been completed. Also, there would be a cap placed on the amount of funds made accessible to a participant through a savings account. In other words, a person could have millions of dollars in the bank, but the savings account available to them, for the entire duration of their participation in the program, would be limited to one year's salary, after taxes, provided by federal minimum wage. If federal minimum wage is $10 per hour and the combination of standard state and federal income taxes is 20% of the total annual income, then all participants would be allowed to deposit no more than a total of $16,640 into the only savings and checking accounts that will remain accessible. Once the program begins, the only deposits that can be made into that savings account will come from the program itself.

Frozen Credit

Depending on your situation, this is either a huge benefit or a significant disadvantage. Every participant's credit would be frozen at the moment of acceptance. All lines of credit would be automatically closed and all debts would be officially handled by employees of the GWP. This will extend to every financial account bearing the individual's name for any reason. In the case of investment or savings accounts, they will remain inaccessible while continuing to collect interest.

Currently our financial and credit systems do not provide for the following scenario, but the idea is as follows:

> Effectively, any financial institution that extends a line of credit to an individual whose credit has been frozen would be fully responsible for that debt. While the individual who received the credit may face criminal charges (depending on the circumstances) it is ultimately the responsibility of the financial institution to check the credit rating and status of every person submitting an application. Credit extended to a frozen account is tantamount to handing out a prize or a gift and, in most cases, the recipient will not be considered at fault.

This translates into a cash-only lifestyle. No credit card or loan-based purchases would be possible. If the individual does not have the cash to cover the cost of an expense, then he or she must either go without or convince the case worker this is an emergency situation. If it truly is an emergency, then it may be possible to secure funds through the program or access the participant's private frozen accounts.

While participation in the program should improve an individual's overall credit rating, and the elimination of debt will make the account fall into a lower-risk category overall, the account will clearly indicate four years of frozen credit and participation in a debt reduction program. All of this information will remain on an individual's credit report for the standard seven to ten years currently used in bankruptcy cases.

Long-Term Credit Freeze

In cases where involvement is due to out of control debt, then the bankruptcy court may choose to extend the credit freeze for a reasonable period of time beyond the program's completion. This is an extreme decision that goes above and beyond what should be considered necessary in most cases.

Reasonable Reduction

It is reasonable to assume that an individual would be able to purchase some portion of food, clothes and other basic necessities on sale, in discount stores or used. Therefore, the amount of funds provided would be based on the true cost of living minus a reasonable percentage. For example, if a family of four can expect to spend $500 per month on food at standard retail prices, but it is reasonable to expect that the use of coupons, sale prices and other community resources will reduce that budget by 10%, then each family of four would be provided with $450.

The challenge would be in identifying a reasonable reduction, particularly when the services of local non-profits are being included in the reduction. When it is assumed that a non-profit will reduce the overall costs of every family involved, it is also assumed that non-profit will maintain consistent funding, resources and services. As recent struggles with the economy have illustrated, non-profits are not necessarily a reliable constant.

Penny Pincher's Reward

An option for budget reduction that might prove more effective than forced reliance on non-profit resources is to provide a reward to participants who remain under budget. For example, if the total amount of SNAP (formerly food stamps) and spending money provided to a family of four is about $3000 per month and that family actually spends $2000, half of the remaining funds could be added to the entertainment fund – in this case, that would increase the entertainment fund by $500.

If food, clothes and incidents are all provided on the EBT card, and those purchases are subject to specific limitations (e.g.: no cigarettes or alcohol) and restricted to participating stores, then moving the remaining money to the entertainment fund's debit card (or prepaid credit card) is the same as providing half of the remaining funds in cash.

Everyone Qualifies

While this program is geared toward helping people struggling with poverty and unemployment, the only requirement for participation is valid US Citizenship or legal residency.

Residency Requirements

There are none. When a person needs a job, a place to live, and other basic necessities, forcing them to wait 30 days for residency requirements is unnecessary, counterproductive and illogical. Ideally, the program would be able to provide work, housing and assistance for every person who walks through the door, regardless of legal residency status.

Giving Newcomers an Honest Opportunity

Many people are distrustful of individuals or families who have recently moved to an area, particularly if they are homeless, unemployed or working low-wage jobs. This is an understandable stereotype formed from bad experiences with people actively living a criminal lifestyle. Unfortunately, it unfairly penalizes honest people going through tough times or living a semi-nomadic lifestyle.

This proposed program would provide newcomers an opportunity to prove themselves to be honest, hardworking and reliable people. It is also an opportunity for area small businesses and non-profits to give people they do not know a chance to fill a need and positively contribute to the community.

Dual Income Household

Every participant in the program is provided with an income and benefits that make establishing and maintaining a middle class lifestyle possible. If an individual has a spouse who is also employed, this should not and will not affect the benefits received. However, it is possible that the amount paid toward housing, utilities, clothes, education and other expenses will actually cover only a portion of the total bill. In other words, a second income could potentially make it possible for a family to live in a more expensive house or pay for a private education.

In most cases, an individual will not enter the program unless there is a problem with debt or poverty because having all credit frozen, handing over control of all finances, and submitting to visits from professionals conducting random and routine inspections of any and all aspects of your life is both invasive and restrictive. If a family is simply looking for enough extra income to cover additional expenses, then a non-working spouse would (most likely) go looking for a job in the usual manner.

Court Ordered Participation

For most people, participation in the GWP is voluntary. The exceptions to this rule would include recently released criminals, unemployed criminals currently on probation, individuals who are behind on child support payments, and individuals declaring bankruptcy. In short, the court system can require participation. Also, individuals applying for benefits through human services (aka: welfare) may be directed to participate in the GWP before (or instead of) being supplied traditional assistance.

How GWP Affects Employers

Job Sources

There are two categories of people who enter this program: 1) people who already have jobs and choose to keep them, and 2) people who are unemployed or in the process of changing employment.

Large corporations and businesses that employ a certain number of workers are not eligible for participation in the position-search aspect of this program. In those cases, only existing, permanent, full-time, employees are eligible.

Small Business and Agricultural Subsidy

Because the program ensures all of the necessities for an entire household are covered, while providing a unique set of benefits, it acts as a subsidy paid directly to the employees of target businesses, such as:

1. Farming and agriculture
2. Non-profit organizations
3. Schools and education
4. Small businesses
5. State parks, national parks and similar government organizations

Each business and organization would have to complete a standardized application process. After the paperwork is reviewed and approved, the program would provide a total number of employees and an annual salary. For example: 1) ten full-time, year-round, employees at $10 per hour or $20,800 per year, or 2) 20 full-time, seasonal, employees at $10 per hour or $5,200 quarterly.

Agricultural Grants

In the case of small family farms in need of a large number of seasonal workers, the program would work directly with immigration as well as local non-profits, businesses and residents to find the necessary help. In this way, agricultural needs are being addressed while problems with illegal immigration are avoided and all workers are provided a fair wage, benefits and the legal protections due to all human beings.

The program would provide workers to area farms for free or at significantly reduced rates. This kind of quote might look something like this: 100 full-time workers at $10,000 per month ($100 per worker) for three months, for a grand total of $30,000 for the entire harvest.

Non-Profit and Government Grants

Similar to the current AmeriCorps program, non-profit businesses could apply for assistance through this program and receive a set number of workers free of charge or for a significantly lower hourly wage than would otherwise be paid. These grants would be available to all qualifying non-profits and government agencies such as the National Park Service or a city's Park and Recreation department.

Professional Employment

Individuals with exceptional professional skills who enter the program unemployed may be eligible for special higher-paying professional positions secured through the program. For example, a pediatrician may enter the program unemployed and directly out of medical school. The case worker could potentially place the doctor at a non-profit medical facility for an hourly rate that is significantly higher than the rate charged for janitorial and office workers.

In these cases, the situation would be handled as if the participant had entered the program already employed. The household budget would take all wages into consideration and may include program fees (SEE: Paying Into The Program).

Unemployment

This program will not replace the existing unemployment benefits system. However, it will stand as an option available to individuals who were unable to find work in the traditional manner before their unemployment benefits ran out. It may also help to provide more accurate data on the number of people who are truly unemployed at any given time.

Paying Into the GWP

As an additional source of revenue for supporting the GWP, there would be times when specific participants and employers would be required to pay into the program.

Individuals

People who enter the program with steady employment may be receiving a paycheck that is significantly larger than the pay provided by jobs supplied through the program. In these cases, the household budget may include a program fee based on a percentage of total income.

A chart detailing reasonable participations fees paid by individuals would have to be drawn up. This will involve identifying reasonable percentages based on total annual income. The end result will look something like the calculations presented in the following illustration.

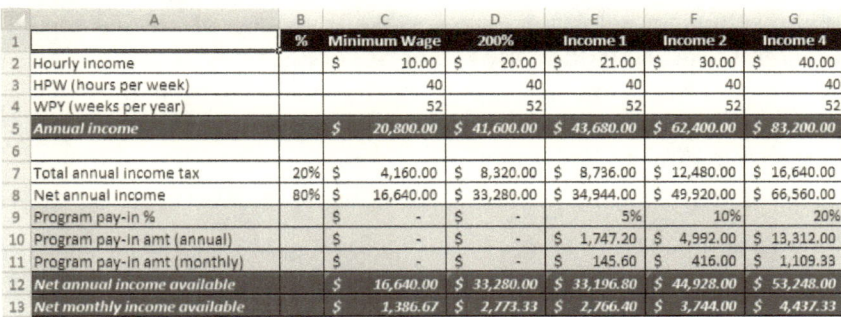

	A	B	C	D	E	F	G
		%	Minimum Wage	200%	Income 1	Income 2	Income 4
1							
2	Hourly income		$ 10.00	$ 20.00	$ 21.00	$ 30.00	$ 40.00
3	HPW (hours per week)		40	40	40	40	40
4	WPY (weeks per year)		52	52	52	52	52
5	*Annual income*		$ 20,800.00	$ 41,600.00	$ 43,680.00	$ 62,400.00	$ 83,200.00
6							
7	Total annual income tax	20%	$ 4,160.00	$ 8,320.00	$ 8,736.00	$ 12,480.00	$ 16,640.00
8	Net annual income	80%	$ 16,640.00	$ 33,280.00	$ 34,944.00	$ 49,920.00	$ 66,560.00
9	Program pay-in %		$ -	$ -	5%	10%	20%
10	Program pay-in amt (annual)		$ -	$ -	$ 1,747.20	$ 4,992.00	$ 13,312.00
11	Program pay-in amt (monthly)		$ -	$ -	$ 145.60	$ 416.00	$ 1,109.33
12	*Net annual income available*		$ 16,640.00	$ 33,280.00	$ 33,196.80	$ 44,928.00	$ 53,248.00
13	*Net monthly income available*		$ 1,386.67	$ 2,773.33	$ 2,766.40	$ 3,744.00	$ 4,437.33

As this sample budget shows, the amount paid into the program increases as the annual income increases. Anything above 200% of minimum wage would have some portion of income designated for payment of program fees. The percentage of income would be no greater than 20%.

Participating Employers

Most small businesses, non-profit organizations and agricultural companies will pay wages for the employees supplied. Each employer's needs and financial situation would be evaluated during the application process and a contract would be drawn up detailing the number of employees, the job descriptions and the company's financial obligation.

The amount paid per hour, per season or per project will vary greatly from one agreement to the next. Also, there would be a set amount of funds set aside for use as employment grants, allowing for the possibility of providing workers at little to no cost.

Large Corporations

The Dishwasher's Law may be written with a provision allowing large corporations the option of voluntarily paying into the Financial Damages Fund (FDF) in exchange for the privileges of providing all employees with a benefits package through the GWP. Enrollment in the GWP would not be required for employees choosing to take advantages of the benefits package.

The Financial Damages Fund (FDF)

There are several large and successful companies that are well known for consistently and habitually paying extremely low wages. Wal-Mart is also known for helping employees take advantage of existing programs, like SNAP (formerly known as Food Stamps) as a supplement to the low wages provided by the company. In these cases, many employees will, most likely, find themselves participating in the GWP through bankruptcy-related court-order or voluntarily choosing to participate before reaching the point of bankruptcy.

When a company is too large to qualify for standard participation in the GWP, but consistently pays wages so low that a significant number of its employees are forced to rely on government programs, then it is effectively using tax-funded human services programs to supplement wages and benefits. This drains standard human services programs of limited resources and steals subsidies intended to assist small businesses and organizations that are not realistically capable of paying a living wage -- like those described in this proposed GWP.

No employer is automatically required to pay into the GWP through the Financial Damages Fund described in chapter two. However, systemic abuse of the resources provided by tax-funded human services programs and habitual disregard for the safety and basic needs of employees may result in a lawsuit. The court system will then decide what actions would be taken, including potential fines and mandatory FDF payments.

In this way, large corporations will either increase wages to an amount that covers the true cost of living, or they will face the possibility of paying an annual fee for the privilege of utilizing resources provided by any number of tax-funded human services programs.

More information on pay-in requirements for businesses can be found in chapter two: The Dishwasher's Law.

Basics and Benefits in Detail

When providing charitable assistance it can be easy to fall into the trap of thinking people need to just take whatever they are given. It is imperative that the attitude and approach toward GWP participants is one of problem solving and assistance provided to an equal. Also, it can be difficult for a parent to focus on the job at hand when the following problems exist at home: 1) his or her child is unable to join the band at school because the cost of the uniform is prohibitive, or 2) the entire family lives in an apartment without furniture or a complete set of dishes and cookware.

The objective is to ensure that the basics are covered and the family's needs are met for as long as the participant shows up for work, stays out of trouble, and does whatever he or she is supposed to do. By assessing all aspects of the living situation and addressing needs in a positive and constructive way, the program helps to keep stress levels intact and employees properly focused.

Therefore, every person would receive the amount needed to cover all dependants in the household, regardless of family size or circumstance. It may be necessary for a case worker to verify the complete dependant list but, once approved, the total amount budgeted would be built around the needs of the entire household.

Clothing

The clothing budget must be realistic. If a participant is working construction or a manual labor job that requires a uniform, the appropriate clothes and shoes must be supplied. Alternately, if the individual is working in an office that requires a professional appearance, the appropriate clothes and shoes must also be supplied. This is particularly important if the individual does not already have a basic professional wardrobe, because getting it established will (most likely) require a combination of new and used items.

The fact that a local charity has a room full of used clothes available to poor people, does not, necessarily, mean that a person would be able to find an outfit that is both the correct size and suited to his or her professional (or personal) needs.

Special allowances must also be made for pregnant women, children and people who either lose or gain a large amount of weight during the course of their work. In most cases this will not be an issue, but when it happens, an individual has no choice but to replace all or most of his or her wardrobe. Therefore, it would be prudent to build in provisions for pregnant women and children, and base the management of other size-changing scenarios off of the same system.

After the initial work wardrobe is in place, the clothing budget will consist of a reasonable monthly allowance for the entire family. In addition, the budget will incorporate special funding for school clothes, school uniforms, camp uniforms, and similar expenses generally incurred by children.

Communication

Cell phones and internet access are no longer luxury items. An enormous amount of communication is completed through email and websites. Employers, child care providers, schools, and many other individuals and organizations expect an individual to remain easily accessible via a cell phone, email and even text messaging. Landline phones are becoming less common, but they are extremely useful in emergency situations.

Access

This includes all of the following: a cell phone for daily communication, a landline for potential emergencies, and internet access for email, video conferencing, online class work, informational websites, etc.

Equipment

The challenge will come in identifying and securing the necessary equipment. Depending on the needs of the individual or family, it may be necessary to secure new cell phones, new computer equipment, good quality used equipment, or other miscellaneous items to create a workable system.

Child Care, Education and Educational Supplies

Child care, school supplies, school fees, sports fees, music or art lessons, fees for extracurricular activities, summer camps and tutors or additional expenses for special needs students are all important and reasonable expenses to be considered. Every participant would have the basic child care and educational needs for every child in the household covered.

Depending on the circumstances, a case worker may require some form of proof the children are having their needs properly addressed. In most cases, the first priority will consist of securing childcare for very young children and ensuring school aged children have everything they need to either begin or continue their schooling. Also, a case worker may need to look into relocating the family or arranging for a private school in cases where there are concerns about the childcare or school system available.

The program should have some sort of fund available for extracurricular activities such as music lessons, art lessons, girl scouts, boy scouts, 4-H, little league, summer camp, sports teams, and so on. While the budget may be limited, it is necessary because these experiences directly influence a child's social and academic development. This also allows a child to participate in the community – just like any other kid.

Debt Repayment

One of the advantages to participating in this program is the ability to address all debts, including:

1. Automobile loans
2. Business loans and debts
3. Child support
4. Court fees
5. Credit card debt
6. Legal fines
7. Medical bills
8. Mortgages and back rent

9. Private loans
10. Student loans
11. Taxes
12. Utilities bills

As soon as an individual is accepted into the program, all collection efforts, fees and interest must stop. Accounts are frozen, credit is frozen, and responsibility for money management transfers to the GWP, which will then assign employees to act as the official points of contact.

If a person already has a good paying job, then a budget would be created around that salary. This can help to increase the total amount that can reasonably be paid over four years. However, there is always a limit to the amount of debt that can be paid. Depending on the size and nature of the debts owed, a participant may be referred to a bankruptcy attorney.

There are three items that can be reduced, but not eliminated, to help address debt-reduction problems: 1) entertainment fund, 2) investment fund and 3) retirement fund. In cases where the debt is repaid before the four-year commitment is completed, the GWP will automatically convert to a standard arrangement, with the primary focus moving to the investment fund. In other words, if $1,200 per month was being used to pay off debts, once the debts are paid that $1,200 would be divided between the entertainment, investment and retirement funds, with the bulk of the payment being deposited in the investment fund.

Entertainment Fund

Everyone needs to spend time having fun with friends and family, which is why every family budget should have a set amount of money put aside for entertainment. The budget provided through this program is no different. A small amount of money is provided each month to cover low-budget activities, such as joining a baseball league, going out for pizza a few times per month, or purchasing birthday or holiday gifts.

This allows individuals to get out into the community and have a good time without having to borrow money from friends or conspicuously refuse to order anything more than a glass of water at a local restaurant. It also helps participants develop the habit of devoting a specific amount of money to those items and activities that qualify as entertainment.

Another option provided by the entertainment fund is the selection of different payment options. A participant can choose to receive the entertainment payment at the same time as all of the other monthly (or bi-weekly) funds. Or, the payment can be made in three, six or twelve month lump sums, which may prove useful for families planning to put that money toward birthday gifts, holiday gifts, or a family vacation.

Training

The monthly statement is designed to act as a training tool. Every participant receives a budget showing the amount of money they make per month and where that money goes. This statement clearly details the amount earned, the remaining debt owed, the amount of money available in various funds, and the total balanced in investment and retirement accounts.

If a client has specific rights or responsibilities tied to the payment of a debt, then those details would be outlined in the monthly budget. For example: A convicted criminal may lose the right to vote if all legal fines and fees are not paid by a certain date. If those fees are being paid through this program, the total amount owed and the date it is due would be clearly listed on the monthly budget.

Depending on the situation, some participants may be required to receive additional training in budgeting or job skills before completing the program. All classes are open to all participants, regardless of circumstances. Here are some examples of training offered through the program:

- **Budgeting for Business** – The basics of accounting and budgeting for a small business.
- **Budgeting for Education** – How to create a reasonable budget for a student attending an institution of higher learning. The objective is to help each person address the specific needs of their family while attending school after completing the program. Also, the educational award is intended to cover all expenses and this class helps to explain how.

- **Budgeting for Home** -- Participants will attend classes that explain how the program's household budgets are created, how household budgets are supposed to work, and where the totals for each category come from (e.g.: 10% into savings). For privacy purposes, classes are based on the standard amount paid to participants who are not already employed when entering the program.
- **Business Plans** – This class is required of all participants choosing the business startup investment option because a solid business plan must be available before the participant can access the funds in the investment account.
- **Job Skills** – Available to participants according to need and interest, these classes cover everything from communication skills to computer skills.

Food, Household Supplies and Incidentals

Currently, human services departments hand out EBT cards, which provides funding for food and incidentals, with restrictions on purchases built into the electronic system managing the cards. Utilizing this same system, the GWP would cover all basic necessities required to maintain a household. This also means the existing restrictions on purchases of non-approved products, such as alcohol and cigarettes, would still apply.

Housing and Utilities

Rent, mortgage and utilities would be paid directly through the program. In this way, all expenses would be covered fully and on-time. However, these expenses must remain within reason. When the cost of housing and utilities is beyond what the program can cover, a case worker may request assistance in any of the following: 1) relocating a family into a better living situation, 2) energy efficiency updating of the participant's home, and 3) repairs to the windows, roof and other aspects of the participant's home.

Homeless

When a person enters the program homeless, the first priority is securing appropriate permanent housing. This applies to all forms of homelessness, including living out of a vehicle, staying with friends or family, living in a hotel, and staying at a homeless shelter. Since moving a participant is significantly harder once they've started working, it is important to identify a suitable living situation at the outset.

Not Homeless

When families already have a home, the desire to remain is often an emotional one. Also, in many areas finding a new home is so difficult it is often more realistic for a family to remain where they are. Every case worker must handle each housing concern on a case-by-case basis, keeping in mind both budget requirements and the reasonable needs and concerns of the family involved.

If a participant is already living in a house or apartment, keeping the family in the current home is a priority. However, there is a limit to the amount of money that can be paid toward rent, utilities and property taxes. If the cost of staying in the home is simply more than can be covered through the program, the family would have to be moved to a more reasonable location. By the same token, if the number and cost of repairs needed to make the home safe, livable, and cost effective are more than can be covered through the program, the family would have to be relocated.

When a participant enters the program with a job or has a home that is entirely paid for, the ability to pay for a more expensive home or apartment increases. Also, a participant can choose to pay for rent or a mortgage with their own personal savings, as long as the total amount needed to cover these costs falls within the program restrictions on the amount of savings that are accessible to participants.

Rent to Own

Whenever possible, the GWP will work with organizations like Habitat for Humanity and devote a set amount of funding toward the purchase, repair, and update of existing homes. These homes will then be made available to participants in need of housing on a rent-to-own basis. Priority would be given to individuals with children who have elected to put their investment fund toward the purchase of a home. In this way, the monthly payments will reduce the total cost of the home and the investment fund will further reduce the total purchase price. By the time the program has been completed, the total mortgage needed to purchase the house would be significantly more affordable.

Relocating for Better Housing

Sometimes individuals and families need to get out of a bad living situation. This could be because of the poor condition of the housing, the people living in the home, or the surrounding neighborhood. Regardless of the reason, if a participant needs to relocate, then securing better housing is the first priority.

Home Repair and Updating

If the costs of utilities in a home or apartment are too high, then weatherization and other repairs may be in order. This is when home inspections are particularly useful because the first question that must be answered is whether or not it is financially feasible to cover the costs of repairs in the interests of reducing the overall costs of utilities.

Also, when a family owns a home, there are going to be times when repairs would have to be made. Since all costs are covered, there would be a fund to address any and all necessary repairs. This is in addition to the costs that are covered by homeowners or renters insurance.

Insurance

The participant and all members of the household would be covered through the following forms of insurance: health, life, home and auto. The premiums on these policies would be paid directly to the insurance company.

Investment Fund

The following categories are the standard objectives most participants would be focused on achieving. It is possible other options may arise and case-workers would be expected to address these objectives on a case-by-case basis.

Car

The objective is to buy a reliable vehicle without taking out a loan.

Education

This is the only benefit that is financially flexible. The benefit covers the total costs involved in completing a degree or specialized training. Because the total costs may vary, depending on the school a student is accepted into, this benefit operates more like a scholarship than a standard investment fund.

House

The most common use of this fund will most likely consist of a down payment on a new home. However, it could be used to raise the money needed to make significant changes to an existing home.

Small Business

Pulling together start-up costs is often the single most challenging hurdle entrepreneurs' face. This benefit helps small businesses get passed that hurdle.

Relocation Allowance

If an area simply has more workers than work, or if a participant has skills that are in high demand elsewhere, then a case worker can access funds for relocating new participants. This would be particularly useful when placing young adults, college students, single adults without children, and people who tend to live a transient lifestyle. In short, if a person is both willing and able to move to another location for the purpose of taking a job, the program would have the resources available to assist in making that move.

Retirement Fund

Little more than a social security supplement, it is intended to provide a person the same basic lifestyle that the GWP provides all participants. These funds are inaccessible before retirement. There is no option to cash out or draw on these funds until the age of 55.

However, if a person takes a permanent job outside of the program, they are provided the option of continuing to make deposits into this fund. Regardless of whether the individual or the program contributes to the fund, it remains inaccessible until the participant reaches the age of 55.

Taxes

Every financial detail necessary for filing taxes is either supplied to or managed through the program. Therefore, every case worker should be able to press a button and print out a completed 1040 or 1040ex tax form, ready for the participant to sign. This form could be used, as is, by any and all participants who do not have additional special considerations, such as: investment income, self-employment or second job income, taxable gifts, gambling or lottery winnings, or an inheritance.

Because the far majority of the participants will not have additional considerations, the program will provide either on-staff tax accountants or a special fund for the purpose of addressing tax related issues. A case worker must submit paperwork requesting access to these resources on a case by case basis.

Transportation

The ability to get to work, school and area businesses varies greatly from one person to the next. It is extremely important to recognize that the existence of a public transportation system does not, necessarily, eliminate the need for access to a reliable vehicle.

Time

Spending an unreasonable amount of time and energy on a commute, grocery shopping or other necessary tasks reduces the amount of time spent with families, friends and (most importantly) children. As a general rule, a commute lasting longer than an hour presents an unreasonable hardship and is hard evidence that existing transportation options are not meeting the individual's basic needs.

Vehicles

In some cases, addressing the problem may involve securing a private vehicle, fixing an existing vehicle, moving to an apartment in a more accessible location, or arranging some kind of rideshare with a coworker. It is up to the caseworker to assist in troubleshooting the issue and identifying a realistic solution.

Vacation

Vacation time consists of one to two weeks of paid time-off. Individuals who are working part-time or seasonal jobs will not be eligible for vacation benefits.

There are no special vacation funds put aside or provided, which means individuals who manage to take an expensive vacation had the money in the bank before beginning the program, found another person kind enough to pay for practically everything, or successfully managed to save every last penny of the monthly entertainment fund.

Special Cases

Bankruptcy

One of the advantages to the GWP is the opportunity to provide individuals facing bankruptcy with an additional option for addressing debt. As a general rule, any debt that cannot be addressed during four years of participation in the GWP is eligible for discharge through bankruptcy. Also, while participation would be recorded on a credit report, it will not have the same negative effect as a bankruptcy on the overall credit score.

Universal Debt Limits

All participants supplied a job through the program receive the exact same hourly wage, regardless of the work being performed. This limits the amount of debt that can be eliminated through the debt-reduction benefit. However, if a participant is already employed and chooses to take advantage of the debt-reduction benefit then the entire salary provided by the current employer would be utilized. A unique budget would be created, which may or may not require selling a home, moving into a less expensive apartment, or providing additional family members with jobs. The amount of debt that can be addressed will depend on the total household income available.

Example Calculation

A possible calculation of the total benefit allowed is as follows: If the federal minimum wage is $10 per hour, standard state and federal taxes are 20% of the total annual income, all other expenses are covered, 80% of after-tax income is applied toward debt, and an individual works 40 hours per week, then the total after-tax amount available for debt reduction is about $13,000 per year or about $53,000 over 4 years.

The following spreadsheet provides further illustration and detail:

	A	B %	C Minimum Wage	D 200%	E Income 1	F Income 2	G Income 4
1							
2	Hourly income		$ 10.00	$ 20.00	$ 21.00	$ 30.00	$ 40.00
3	HPW (hours per week)		40	40	40	40	40
4	WPY (weeks per year)		52	52	52	52	52
5	*Annual income*		$ 20,800.00	$ 41,600.00	$ 43,680.00	$ 62,400.00	$ 83,200.00
6							
7	Total annual income tax	20%	$ 4,160.00	$ 8,320.00	$ 8,736.00	$ 12,480.00	$ 16,640.00
8	Net annual income	80%	$ 16,640.00	$ 33,280.00	$ 34,944.00	$ 49,920.00	$ 66,560.00
9	Program pay-in %		$ -	$ -	5%	10%	20%
10	Program pay-in amt (annual)		$ -	$ -	$ 1,747.20	$ 4,992.00	$ 13,312.00
11	Program pay-in amt (monthly)		$ -	$ -	$ 145.60	$ 416.00	$ 1,109.33
12	*Net annual income available*		$ 16,640.00	$ 33,280.00	$ 33,196.80	$ 44,928.00	$ 53,248.00
13	*Net monthly income available*		$ 1,386.67	$ 2,773.33	$ 2,766.40	$ 3,744.00	$ 4,437.33
20	**Debt Reduction Benefits (Annual)**						
21	Debt Reduction	80%	$ 13,312.00	$ 26,624.00	$ 26,557.44	$ 35,942.40	$ 42,598.40
22	Retirement	2%	$ 332.80	$ 665.60	$ 663.94	$ 898.56	$ 1,064.96
23	Entertainment	5%	$ 832.00	$ 1,664.00	$ 1,659.84	$ 2,246.40	$ 2,662.40
24	Investment	3%	$ 499.20	$ 998.40	$ 995.90	$ 1,347.84	$ 1,597.44
25	*4-year debt repayment cap*		$ 53,248.00	$ 106,496.00	$ 106,229.76	$ 143,769.60	$ 170,393.60

The total amount of money that can be discharged through the debt-reduction benefit, when the job is provided by the program, would be clearly and publically available. If that number is $53,000, then the credit card companies and banks would be responsible for ensuring that any loans made in larger amounts would be covered by other resources. Anything above $53,000 would be considered a loss if the individual enters the GWP without an existing and reliable income significantly higher than the program's baseline. Conversely, an individual with an income below the program's baseline would have the ability to eliminate more debt, without declaring bankruptcy, then his or her income would generally allow.

Financial Organization Benefits

No matter who you are, what your credit rating may be, or how much money you make, the minimum wage debt repayment cap is the minimum amount of credit available to you. Simply put, if this program were established nation-wide, every U.S. citizen and legal resident would be able to borrow up to the minimum debt reduction amount. This creates a situation where raising the minimum wage is in the best interests of financial institutions and other lenders, because it increases the number of people who can borrow that amount of money, while reducing the risk associated with customer default.

New Form of Bankruptcy

This creates an option that falls between being able to pay all bills and being forced to liquidate everything. The bankruptcy court can order participation in the GP. It can also require individuals who make more than 200% of minimum wage to continue paying on a reasonable amount of remaining debt, after the program has been completed. Bankruptcy lawyers may utilize these options to protect assets or property that would otherwise face liquidation in a standard bankruptcy.

For example: Entering the GWP to deal with out of control debt does not, necessarily, protect all assets from liquidation. Bankruptcy lawyers may be able to negotiate a combination of actions to address the majority of an individual's debt. For example, if a person has several assets including a family farm, a savings account, a retirement account and a handful of family heirlooms, everything except the savings account could, potentially, be declared a protected asset. If creditors are trying to force the sale of some of these items, then participation in the GWP may help to secure the protection of those items in bankruptcy court.

Court Ordered Long-Term Credit Cap

In cases where the individual has declared bankruptcy multiple times due to mismanagement of funds or medically diagnosed mental illness, the court can restrict credit extensions to the maximum amount that can be paid through participation in the program, regardless of how much money the individual has saved or receives through a paycheck, investments, gifts, etc. A hard-cap on credit is clearly noted on the individual's credit report and remains in place for a minimum of 10 years.

Child Support

Falling behind on child support obligations can be devastating because the consequences faced by people who do not pay child support, for any reason, are severe. Individuals who have fallen behind on support payments would be given the option of catching up on payments through the GWP. People who are simply struggling financially would have the option of entering this program to ensure those payments are made. The court system would be able to require participation for the purpose of paying back child support.

Criminal Records

It is unrealistic to assume that any program will eliminate criminal activity. There will always be people who are drawn to that lifestyle and seem to live for breaking the rules. The best change that any program can hope for, is the reduction (or elimination) of the need to commit criminal acts. In other words, provide people with a realistic, legal, option and those who choose to pursue illegal activities anyway are (most likely) making a conscious choice to do so.

Recidivism

Society should do everything in its power to eliminate the need to participate in criminal activity while providing peace keeping forces with the resources necessary to pursue those individuals whose illegal activities are primarily a matter of choice. But, if we are able to remove the people who commit crimes due to the realities of living in poverty, then the court system and the police would be able to focus available resources on those who are consciously choosing to participate in criminal activity and those who are struggling with some form of mental illness.

The GWP provides an excellent vehicle for providing an apartment and a job to people who were recently released from prison or are struggling to find work due to a criminal record. As long as a person show up for work, payments on all debts (including child support, court fees, fines, taxes, etc) would be kept current and paid directly to creditors. The individual can trust that he or she would have a place to live, all basic necessities covered, and a few dollars to spend on something fun. In short, life would be simple and funds would be tight, but as long as the person shows up for work, does everything he or she is supposed to do, and stays out of trouble, everything will work out all right. Conversely, if a participant chooses to return to a life of crime, the court system will (most likely) judge that person harshly.

Database Search Functions

The unique issues facing individuals who are on probation or living with a criminal history must be specifically addressed in the database of available jobs. The search functions must allow for the input of legal restrictions, qualifications based on criminal history, and things that must be avoided. If a probation officer is already involved, it may make more sense to provide him or her with access to the job database and the power to act as a case worker through this program. Some unique issues that an individual on probation may need to consider when establishing housing and employment:

1. **Family complications** – Based on current issues and a lifetime of history, should this person be allowed to live with family?
2. **Job restrictions** – What kind of job is this person qualified to work? Are there special considerations that a potential employer may not know about? Are there legal restrictions, based on criminal history?
3. **Neighborhood avoidance** – Are there certain areas that this person should avoid at all costs?
4. **Restriction of movement** – Are they wearing an ankle bracelet? How far will the bracelet allow them to move and in what areas?

These search functions should be made available to all case workers because they will most likely prove useful to everyone. For example, the ability to restrict a search by a geographic region of any size or shape is extremely useful when a participant is dependent on public transportation or otherwise limited in mobility.

Immigrants

This program is an excellent way to get recent immigrants transitioned into their new lives in the United States. The combination of security and on-the-job experience will help individuals with a wide range of skills and challenges acclimate themselves to their new home while establishing a verifiable work record. It will also provide an excellent opportunity to secure the funding need for purchasing a home or opening a family business.

Life Changes

Everyone faces changes in life, some more severe than others. It is not unreasonable to expect that a person might want, or need, to simplify his or her work life in order to address more personal issues.

Disabilities and other medical issues

People who have been disabled and have had to learn a new way of both living and working, can utilize this program to reintroduce themselves into the workforce after a long absence. This also provides a much needed option to people who need to change their work environment for reasons involving physical health, repetitive stress injuries, mental health, substance abuse, or the effects of dealing with a hostile work environment.

It's been a while

Stay-at-home parents and other people who have been out of the workforce for a long time may find this program particularly advantageous, due to the opportunity for on-the-job training and the establishment of a current work record. This also allows participants to try something new, meet new people, and explore a field or career path before pursuing potentially expensive training.

My job is gone

Many people who are laid off are unable to find the same kind of work elsewhere because the field has changed, the job no longer exists, or the competition is to fierce. The person is left trying to identify a different but realistic direction to take his or her career. The GWP may be able to help identify a new direction through on-the-job training or experience working alternate jobs (or industries) but utilizing similar skills.

Long Term Participants

It's possible that a participant will reach the end of his or her four-year commitment and choose to sign on with the same job, same benefits and same arrangement for four more years. Some individuals would be working to increase the funding available for going to school or starting a business, particularly if the first four years were focused primarily on debt reduction. Other people will simply decide this is the perfect job and the perfect lifestyle!

While this may seem like a radical concept, I would strongly suggest that both possibilities are reasonable and provisions must be put into place to accommodate a wide variety of scenarios. For example:

1. A retired factory worker enters the program to keep active and address the debts incurred during his late wife's illness. After four years, the debt is entirely under control and he is given the option of living solely on social security or continuing the program. He likes his job with the city park service and chooses to continue. Four more years go by and he has a healthy investment fund started, with no plans for either starting a business or going to school. In fact, he makes it clear to his case worker that he would prefer to keep working his city park job for as long as he is able simply because he likes the work and the people. So, the case worker and client work out a plan to provide the investment fund to his grandchildren in the form of college scholarships.

2. A single mother in her early 20s enters the program to deal with a small debt problem and secure funds for school. After four years, she enters college with all expenses paid, including housing, childcare, food, and insurance. Unfortunately, completing college does not guarantee a job and the young woman re-enters the program. Her case worker helps to identify career goals and attempts to find a job within the program that is either related to those objectives or in the

same field. The investment fund is used to build up for a down payment on a new car or a house. Two years later, the woman finds a job and leaves the program. Her investment fund remains available for the intended purchases. Three years later, the woman accesses those funds and purchases a home.

3. A young man enters the program immediately after high school. He is an artist who spends his entire working life alternating between working through this program to save money for art school and attending art schools throughout the United States and abroad.

4. A young woman enters the program immediately after high school. She works for eight years and still has no real interest in either attending school or starting a business. The case worker converts the investment fund into a home or car fund and the young woman uses it to buy a house, but continues to work the same job. The program covers the cost of the mortgage instead of rent on an apartment (because the house fell within an acceptable price range). Many years later, the woman retires from the same job and continues to live in the same house.

5. A young man graduates high school and enters the program because of the business start-up funding option. He successfully completes four years of work and starts a business. After a few years the business fails and he re-enters the program. After building up more start-up business funds, he launches a second business venture, which also fails. He continues doing this until he finally succeeds with his fourth business.

Mobile Communities

Assuming that all members of a mobile or nomadic community are criminals is both damaging and inaccurate. However, one of the strengths of the GWP is the ability to provide these people with legal options for employment, as well as legal recourse and accessible protection from abusive employers, human traffickers, and other people who prey on vulnerable communities. The benefits provided by the GWP can also help to address problems that arise from uninsured individuals habitually using emergency rooms to address all kinds of medical concerns. This combination of assistance should prove to be helpful to all branches of law enforcement as they work to focus resources on dealing with truly dangerous criminals.

Illegal Immigrants

Regardless of the political atmosphere surrounding immigrants without proper legal paperwork, this is a community of people that provides the United States with a much-needed workforce. Many farms couldn't operate without seasonal workers, small family businesses provide a positive economic influence on local communities, and businesses of all sizes and types utilize their skills. There are those who have been living in this country, as quality employees and productive members of their communities, for many decades.

The establishment of the GWP provides the opportunity to create an amnesty program specifically targeting people who provide a needed service to all kinds of small businesses and farms. Participation would not be based on number of years in the country but on a participating employers' recommendation. Ultimately, the focus should remain on finding ways to separate the dangerous criminals from honest people who came into this country to create a better life for themselves and their families. Giving businesses and workers alike a legal option to continue living their lives will help to separate the good people from the criminals.

The questions that need to be answered include the following:

1. How long will the legal residency last and what happens to the worker when the residency expires?
2. Does the residency extend to an individual's family?
3. Does a criminal record (of any kind) disqualify a person from consideration?
4. How many people can any one employer recommend to this program?
5. Will there be penalties for employers who enter the program with illegal immigrants already on the payroll?

Migrant Workers

Every year, farms and other businesses rely on migrant workers to provide a necessary service. There are some tasks that simply cannot be done with a machine and, frequently, these tasks are seasonal in nature – such as the annual harvest of a wide variety of produce. Clearly, migrant workers provide a necessary service. Unfortunately, this service is often provided to farms and businesses that simply cannot afford to pay regular wages. The GWP would provide the assistance necessary to allow farms and other agricultural businesses access to the necessary manual labor without incurring a cost that would push the business into bankruptcy.

Transients

There are many reasons for living a nomadic lifestyle. Sometimes it's part of a community's culture, and other times it's just a matter of personality and interest. Some people are more adventurous or interested in seeing new places, trying new things and meeting new people. Still others work jobs that require moving from place to place. Providing an easily accessible form of legal employment available to anyone, regardless of legal residency status is far better than pan handling, theft, dealing drugs and prostitution.

Natural Disasters and Other Crises

When a true disaster strikes, simple survival becomes a top priority. The usual methods for getting by no longer apply. Depending on the extent of the disaster, things may remain chaotic and unpredictable for a very long time. While emergency shelters, food, water, clothing and medical supplies are the first priority, it could be argued that establishing some method for returning to a 'normal' lifestyle comes in a close second.

Even if providing a full-time job and all of the benefits allowed under the GWP requires temporarily relocating the majority of the people affected by a natural disaster, it is better than asking people to sit idly by, hoping things will get better.

Loss of a Home

When a fire, flood or other catastrophic event destroys the home and most, if not all, of a family's belongings, securing the basic necessities is a top priority. The GWP would be most beneficial in those situations where the combination of insurance money, whatever income the household was already receiving and additional assistance from friends and family does not cover the cost of establishing a residence, rebuilding a home and replacing property.

Natural Disasters

Natural disasters affect more than buildings and property; they take out infrastructure, destroy businesses and eliminate jobs. When hurricanes, floods, tornadoes, earthquakes, or other catastrophic events destroy everything imaginable, basic survival becomes a top priority. Once enough food, clothing, medical supplies and make-shift shelters have been provided to the area, people are either left with the task of helping to clean-up and rebuild, or waiting for more opportunities to arrive.

Providing the full benefits of the GWP to survivors helps to fund the physical and economic rebuilding of an area while providing participants with constructive full-time jobs. In some ways it's both a psychological and economic assistance, because being given the opportunity to keep busy while knowing that your family is fully taken care of and money is being placed into an investment fund that directly benefits your future, can be an enormous relief during times of crises.

Stalkers

Dealing with a stalker is never easy. Some predators are easy to spot while others are significantly more conniving and manipulative. When repeated attempts to remove the abuser from the lives of the abused have failed, victims can find themselves forced into hiding. Establishing a new identity and remaining out of the reach of a stalker is often further complicated by financial and professional difficulties. Without a reliable income source, it can be extremely difficult to remain in hiding. Also, most abusers are very well aware of the power that money, or a lack-there-of, can provide.

Government agencies and non-profit organizations have been developed to help victims deal with stalkers of all kinds. This proposed program would be a particularly powerful tool when utilized through those organizations because a new identity, work history and reliable income could be established without utilizing online job boards.

Pregnant Women

While it is possible for a woman to work during pregnancy, it's extremely difficult to find a job until after the baby is born. If a woman does not have another child and loses her employment and housing, she will not qualify for the assistance available to families until after the baby is born. In most cases, this means she will remain homeless until after the birth of the child.

Through the GWP, a woman would be provided all basic necessities, regardless of whether or not she is pregnant. Like all other participants, housing and other necessities would be addressed first. Once the basics have been established, she and the case worker will determine the kind of work that can be performed during the remainder of the pregnancy.

Following the birth, the woman would be able to go on maternity leave for up to one year, the standard amount of time currently provided under some state human services programs. During maternity leave, the basic necessities would be covered, but deposits into the investment funds will halt. Also, the program clock will stop, so a four year program with a one year maternity leave will actually last a total of five years. When maternity leave has ended, the case worker will help the new mother locate appropriate childcare before assigning her a job.

Prisoners

Entering prisoners into the GWP, will help to ensure the companies who utilize this workforce are adhering the federal employment law, including paying the minimum hourly wage due to any human being in this country. It will also create an alternative system for covering prisoner expenses, such as housing, food, clothes and medical care.

For people on the outside, payments would be made toward debts, child support, legal fees and any other obligations the prisoner might have. Unlike participants outside of the prison system, prisoners will not have an entertainment fund or an investment fund. However, there would be payments made into a retirement fund, as well as a small amount of money made available through the prison convenience store. In this way, prisoners would have something to fall back on when they are released, particularly if they spend several decades behind bars.

Whistleblowers and Victims of Harassment or Discrimination

It's common knowledge that filing a harassment suit or reporting an employer for illegal or unethical business practices will effectively end a career. For some people it can mean the absolute destruction of their professional reputation and losing the ability to find work in any field.

While the GWP will not salvage or protect a career from the wide-reaching effects of retaliation, it will ensure that the individual is able to find a job and pay the bills.

Youth Under Age 18

While there would be plenty of teenagers looking for a way to earn money for college, the young people who need the GWP the most are at risk youths and street kids. There are very few options available to kids trying to survive on their own. Making this program available to anyone of legal working age establishes an immediately functioning safety net for the most vulnerable and least protected members of our society.

Street Kids

The program would have to be modified to allow time for both work and school. While child protective services would have to get involved in order to evaluate the situation and ensure that everyone is safe, there needs to be enough flexibility to allow a teenager to care for several siblings by taking advantage of all the benefits normally provided to an adult.

Accessibility is a key aspect to this portion of the program. Kids on the street need to be able to walk into a location and know they would be immediately provided a meal, clothes, a shower and a place to sleep. Discussions about employment, benefits, education and family can occur afterwards. One way to achieve this goal is by setting up youth community centers and other safe-areas open to all youth under 18, no questions asked, and dedicating specific case workers to these centers. (SEE: Youth Only Areas, in Chapter three: Targeted Community Centers)

Financial Abuse

In some cases, the teenager is dealing with financial and economic abuse. Parents and legal guardians have the legal right to access and remove all funds in a dependant child's bank account. Some adults will also take a child's social security number and run up debts that become the child's responsibility the moment he or she turns 18. This program would freeze the child's credit report, restricting the ability of a parent, guardian or criminal to establish accounts in the child's name. It would also eliminate the possibility of money saved for college being accessed and used for any other reason.

Another measure that should be taken is the automatic freezing of all credit options associated with a social security number at the moment that number is created. This status would be changed when the following things occur: 1) holder of the social security number reaches an age where credit is legally possible, 2) proof of income can be provided, and 3) the appropriate government office receives a form requesting a change in status. This form must provide a reason for the change and include the signature of the holder or the holder's legal guardian.

Cars and College Funds

As for the teenagers looking for ways to pay for college or purchase a car, the information provided through the school system can include instructions to either visit a youth community center or the program's regular offices. The case worker assigned to assisting these teens will try to determine existing skills, interests, and availability for work before assigning a part-time job.

After graduation, many students may choose to continue with the program on a full-time basis, in order to meet certain financial objectives. If a student wants to start a business or buy a house, full-time participation would be necessary. Also, part-time benefits will not cover all college expenses, particularly if a student has to pay for food, housing, books, clothes and other necessities in addition to tuition. The total amount of the benefit provided after completing four years on a part-time basis must be clearly outlined and compared to the full-time reward in all information provided to students considering the option.

The Military

Many people will read this and assume young people have the ability to join the military and take advantage of the college education fund. This is an inaccurate assumption for a handful of reasons:

1. Not everyone can get into the military. There is a long list of potential disqualifiers that include things like medical conditions, criminal history, psychological profile and even a person's height.
2. Not everyone is suited to the military culture. It is wrong to assume that the military will straighten a person out or make a better person about of him or her. Every year people are discharged early, both honorably and otherwise, because of personality issues. It is a tough, unique and somewhat extreme culture; and there are people who do not have the personality it requires.
3. The G.I. Bill is an admirable program that can be used to pay a significant amount of a student's college tuition, but there are limits and eligibility requirements. It's an excellent resource for people who thrive within a military culture, but it may not be enough of a benefit to realistically motivate individuals who are not suited to that environment.

Chapter 2: The Dishwasher's Law

We've all heard the jokes about people who are unable to pay for a meal in a restaurant and end up spending the evening washing dishes. The proposed addition to our legal system is called The Dishwasher's Law for this reason – if people are unable to pay their bills, they must be given a legal option for working off the debt.

Based On Existing Vaccination Laws

First, allow me to point out that I am not a lawyer or an expert in any aspect of the legal system. It is a matter of sheer happenstance that I discovered the federal laws governing personal injuries caused by vaccinations. My layman's understanding of these laws is as follows: companies that manufacture vaccinations must pay into a fund which is used to cover the cost of damages associated with physical injuries that are a direct result of receiving a vaccination. These payments must be made regardless of whether or not an injury ever occurs.

Vaccines are necessary to the management of public health in the United States and around the globe. However, they come with the inherent risk that a patient may have an adverse reaction that results in bodily harm. Therefore, the companies that manufacture these vaccines must provide financial coverage before the injuries occur. Again, I am not a lawyer, but I would not be surprised to learn there is some kind of beneficial trade-off involving additional protection from personal injury lawsuits that are not found in other areas of medicine.

Financial Damages Fund (FDF)

If the same basic idea is applied to the financial sector, then credit cards, mortgages, car loans and other standard systems of supplying credit to consumers would be the economic equivalent of a vaccination – necessary to the financial health of the general public. In fact, we could take this a step further and say these things are necessary, period. We no longer live in a cash-based society. It is becoming increasingly difficult to conduct day-to-day transactions without a credit or debit card and loans are a crucial element in multiple industries. Therefore it is more than reasonable to require any company that provides services that place people at risk of financial damage to make similar payments into a Financial Damages Fund (FDF).

Voluntary Participation

Some companies may find it cheaper or easier to simply pay the government to handle all health care and benefits. It may be beneficial to include a provision within this law that addresses that option. In this way, employees would receive full health care coverage, retirement fund, child care and any number of the benefits outlined in chapter one, including an EBT card with monthly stipends for food and incidentals. Effectively, the corporation would pay into the program in the same way that it would pay an insurance company or an investment company for the same services. A potential benefit to the employee would be the automatic continuation of these services in the event of unemployment.

If this option is made available, the government body managing the FDF will need to create a department devoted to identifying the options available for purchase, establishing a reasonable price, managing these accounts and providing the appropriate customer service.

Court-Ordered Participation

There are a wide variety of reasons why the courts may choose to order a company to make payments into the Financial Damages Fund. These payments would result from rulings made in lawsuits addressing practices that directly result in current or former employees being forced to rely on human services programs.

While this option is worth discussing, it must be pointed out that it is probably going to be politically unpopular – particularly in reference to companies that have been convicted of hiring illegal immigrants or have participated in sending jobs overseas.

Unfair Business Practices

Any illegal or unethical business practice that destroys healthy competition or puts people out of work may qualify for this penalty. Potentially, these practices could include: 1) Any business practice that unfairly undercuts the competition, such as price gouging, 2) attempting to break up a union, and 3) using vicious rumors and slander to destroy a competitor's business.

Illegal Business Practices

This law would provide additional protection against predatory lending, but it is not designed to replace existing laws addressing illegal and fraudulent activities within the financial and business sectors. White collar crimes would still be subject to all relevant investigations and legal penalties.

That said, the courts may choose to levy additional penalties in the form of restitution payments made directly to the FDF, based on the amount of financial damage caused, the number of people forced into utilizing human services programs, or other relevant factors.

Illegal Hiring and Firing Practices

The law could be written to include provisions for penalties levied against companies who are convicted of operating sweat shops, employing illegal immigrants, breaking child labor laws, actively participating in discriminatory hiring practices, or otherwise breaking laws that governing the hiring and firing of employees. This would include employers who attempt to fire employees who utilize the Guaranteed Work Program (GWP) or other human services programs.

In every case, the company is abusing existing workers while taking away potential jobs from US citizens or legal residents. These practices also frequently force more people to rely on government assistance and increase the number of people utilizing hospital emergency rooms due to a lack of health insurance. Therefore, forcing these companies to pay into the FDF, and the programs it would support, makes sense.

Sending Jobs Overseas

This would be a politically unpopular provision, but it remains worth mentioning. The dishwasher's law could be written to include a provision declaring jobs eliminated in the United States and created in a foreign country as a business practice that qualifies for penalties in the form of payments into the financial damages fund. Essentially, the companies participating in this practice have created a large pool of workers who are forced to rely on unemployment and other government funded programs. Therefore, they would be responsible for covering part of the cost of running those programs.

Another potential legal action which would be equally unpopular among politicians would be the inclusion of payment and benefits provided to foreign workers as a form of unfair business practice. In other words, if a company moves a factory to another country and reduces costs by paying workers less than minimum wage, providing little or no benefits, disregarding environmentally friendly practices, and otherwise participating in unethical actions that would be prohibited in the United States, then those workers *could* be included in the total number of workers utilized in the Corporate Welfare Payments calculation.

Corporate Bankruptcy

Elimination of existing pension plans may pull a company out of bankruptcy and possible closure, but it also places all of those retired employees into the government human services system. Therefore, as part of a bankruptcy case, the court may choose to require a company to pay into the Financial Damages Fund to help alleviate the addition of people who are now reliant on taxpayers' dollars.

Corporate Welfare Payments

The final law would have to establish realistic percentages and guidelines based on the total number of employees working for the company, as well as the total number of employees receiving a wage low enough to be considered eligible for FDF funded programs.

The following illustration provides an overly simplified example of how these numbers might look:

	A	B	C	D
1		Full-Time	Part-Time	Total
2	Gross Taxable Profits			$ 25,000,000.00
3	Total Employees	5,000	10,000	15,000
4	Number of FDF Employees	2,000	4,000	6,000
5	FDF Employees %	40%	40%	40%
6	FDF Eligible Income			$ 10,000,000.00
7	FDF Payment %			10%
8	Financial Damages Fund Pmt			$ 1,000,000.00
9	Cost Per FDF Employee			$ 166.67

In this example: the company is paying 6,000 employees' wages that fall within the FDF range. This consists of 40% of the total number of employees hired, so 40% of the Gross Taxable Profits are eligible for consideration under this law. The guidelines state that 5,000-10,000 total FDF employees requires a payment equal to 10% of the total eligible pre-tax profits. In this case that comes to a total annual payment of $1,000,000 or about $166 per employee.

NOTE: The inclusion of both full-time and part-time employees is necessary in order to prevent companies from avoiding payment by dropping full-time employees down to the maximum number of hours allowed for a part-time employment. Current temporary agencies use this tactic regularly because limiting a worker's schedule to 35 hours per week allows them to maintain 'temporary' positions, without benefits, for longer than one year.

Chapter 3: Targeted Community Centers

What follows is a description of what a targeted community center might look like. My example focuses on services needed by adults, youths and children struggling with homelessness and/or addiction. The same basic idea could be modified to suit the needs of other chronic problems, such as eating disorders, domestic abuse or the annual increase in population due to the arrival of migrant workers.

These centers would be run by non-profit organizations with the following objectives: building and maintaining a facility that provides physical space for non-profit organizations. In other words, the non-profit that builds the center would be devoted entirely to maintaining the building and reducing overall costs in rent and utilities for the non-profits that utilize the space. Depending on the organization behind the building, there may also be an additional focus on establishing additional centers in other areas.

Reduced Duplication of Services

One of the advantages inherent in building a targeted community center is the opportunity to reduce duplication of services provided by different non-profit organizations. In the example provided below, the shelter provides beds and showers, the soup kitchen provides foods and the public library provides internet access and reading materials. In this way, each organization can focus on one piece of the puzzle, ultimately creating a community center that provides a complete list of services needed by a specific community.

Example Targeted Issues: Homelessness and Addiction

Most of this book is devoted to ideas that assist people manage finances, secure jobs, develop small businesses and generally establish or maintain a middle class lifestyle. However, the unfortunate reality is that no program or law will eliminate the need for homeless shelters, psychiatric hospitals, addiction treatment centers or prisons. While we can work to significantly reduce the overall need, there will always be some segment of the population that requires these kinds of services and facilities.

The following description of a potential targeted community center is geared toward addressing the needs of people who struggle with chronic homelessness, while providing access to information and services that can help to break that cycle.

24-Hour Meeting Rooms

The majority of the space in this building would consist of meeting rooms that are available to any and all non-religious 12-step programs on a 24-hour basis.

12-Step Programs

The objective is to have a meeting in every room, 24-hours a day, 365 days a year. To this end, the community center will remain in contact with the governing body of all area 12-step programs, letting them know when space is available. Also, the center will work directly with the people managing individual meetings to collect rent and address problems.

Every meeting held at the center must be part of a locally active and recognized 12-step organization. Loss of support from the 12-step organization will result in the loss of the meeting space. Space will not be provided to religion-based 12-sstep programs because those programs are managed by local churches and can (should) be held in a religious setting.

Complete meeting lists for all 12-step programs are always available in main lobby. The community center may choose to publish a complete schedule of meetings being held at the facility, as well as a list of times when rooms are available.

Community Meetings

Meetings run by non-profits and area organizations working to assist people in poverty may rent space as well, but the 12-step programs take priority.

Auditorium

An auditorium with a stage, dance floor and/or large seating area would be made available for special events, speakers, and performances targeted to the community of people who utilize the center.

Bus Station

Specifically designating space for a commercial bus station has multiple advantages above and beyond the obvious financial benefits that come with securing a regular and reliable tenant.

Local Public Transit

By working with local public transit authorities to incorporate both regular bus service and a ticket counter, the community center becomes more accessible to people who need it. Also, it provides the homeless shelter with easy access to local bus tickets, which can simplify one aspect of a shelter worker's job.

National Bus Lines and Private Bus Companies

Again, attracting national companies like Greyhound, as well as smaller regional bus lines, provides a regular commercial income for the bus hub and ticket counter area of the community center. However, it provides easy access for people who are more transient and, therefore, often in need of assistance from a homeless shelter.

Most importantly, is the opportunity for all of these bus lines to work hand-in-hand with the youth-only area. Ideally, this would be rented out to a non-profit focused entirely on helping homeless and at-risk youth get off the street. By placing one of these non-profits into the youth-only area, and physically positioning that space in a location that is fully visible from the bus hub and ticket station, the center increases the possibility of catching these youths before they are lost to the street. Also, by providing a soup kitchen that is available only to children, youths and families, the center increases the possibility of finding and protecting these people when they are most vulnerable.

It might even become possible to collaborate with the bus companies by providing brochures and other information to be displayed in the front of the bus. Drivers will then have the ability and option to give these brochures to youths and other people traveling into the area.

Community Center Staff

Managing this kind of community center will require a full-time staff that includes a facilities manager, a fundraiser and grant writer, office workers, security and cleaning. Depending on available resources, the community center may also choose to hire a person to manage both the computers and the website.

Convenience Store

The convenience store would have to be owned and operated by an individual or non-profit organization with an excellent understanding of, and respect for, the unique needs of the people using the facility. In many ways, it would look like any other convenience store, with the addition of the basic supplies needed by all 12-step meetings.

It is very important that the store refrain from presenting itself as being affiliated with a specific religion or 12-step program. A targeted community center is established to serve a specific community of people, but that community comes from every imaginable religion, culture, creed, race and lifestyle. Therefore, respecting the variety of people and personalities that utilize the space is an extremely important aspect to managing the store.

Emergency Resources

If enough targeted community centers are built throughout an area, they can then be used as a reliable resource in the event of a region-wide emergency or natural disaster. If the buildings are designed with this additional purpose in mind, they could also be used as bomb shelters or safe and secure areas in the event of a terrorist attack or other forms of biological or chemical warfare.

Everyone assumes safe places will be provided in the event of a disaster or act of war, this is one way to ensure those resources truly are available to everyone living in a specific region.

Emergency Housing

Theoretically, the targeted community center could be designed to include several floors that hold between 1000 and 2000 people, which would provide much needed relief to currently overcrowded shelters.

If the total homeless population were significantly reduced, or if enough targeted community centers were built throughout an area, these spaces could be used as emergency shelter in the event of a natural disaster or other significant emergency.

Emergency Soup Kitchen

One of the biggest advantages to using true emergency resources as homeless shelters and soup kitchens is the maintenance and repair of equipment and continual stocking of food. After all, what use is an emergency shelter equipped with non-working equipment, outdated cans of food and empty canisters of fuel?

Fundraising

A targeted community center is, by necessity, collaboration between multiple non-profit organizations. It also addresses the needs of the poorest and most vulnerable people in our society. Therefore, this presents a perfect opportunity for fundraising events involving faith based organizations, interfaith organizations, and communities of people who might otherwise find themselves uncomfortable supporting the services provided in this center. For example, a church that regularly refuses to provide space for 12-step meetings may be happy to assist in raising funds for a targeted community center.

A grant-writer and fundraiser would be on-staff to help raise money to cover the cost of maintaining all aspects of the building. If enough money is raised to cover maintenance, repairs, and other community center expenses, then additional funding will either be applied toward the creation of another community center or the rent and utilities owed by the existing center's non-profit tenants.

12-Step Meetings

12-step meetings have their own way of determining the amount of rent that would be paid each month. The community center will set a reasonably low baseline for the minimum amount due. When a 12-step group pays more than the amount due for a specific meeting, they would be given the option of either pre-paying their rent or having the extra money evenly applied toward the rent of all other meetings within the same program.

For example, if the amount due is $10 per month and an AA group chooses to pay $20, then the extra $10 will either be placed on account for that particular group, or it would be divided among the ten other AA groups holding regular meetings at the same facility.

Individuals and groups also have the option of making a meeting or 12-step specific donation directly to the office. These donations would be applied directly to the account for that meeting or group of meetings. For example Jane Doe enters the office and makes two donations. The first is a personal donation to an AA group that meets at 2 a.m. on Monday mornings. The second is a rent payment for an AA group that meets at 5 p.m. on Friday nights. The Monday morning donation covers all rent currently owed by that group. The Friday night payment covers the rent due for the next three months. Because the Friday night payment is more than the amount due, Jane informs the office that the group has decide to keep the total amount on account, instead of donating it to all AA meetings currently being held at the facility.

When a meeting closes or is asked to leave the community center for any reason, the credit balance on account is dispersed evenly among all meetings within the same 12-step group. No refunds are given at any time.

Non-profits

The community center conducts fundraisers, writes grants and accepts donations to cover the cost of maintaining the facility. The center will accept donations and funding earmarked for the purpose of covering rent and utilities on behalf of a specific non-profit currently residing in the building. However, the amount of funding that can be accepted in this manner is limited by the number of years left on an organization's lease. Also, the community center will always make funding objectives and limitations very clear – non-profit tenants are responsible for their own operating costs.

Green Buildings & Architectural Contests

If the building is being designed, developed and built from the group up, this presents an excellent opportunity to identify and utilize green materials, green energy and other cost-effective options. For example, if a building has the right location and design, a combination of solar panels and a back-up generator hooked up to the grid can significantly reduce utilities costs.

Because every geographical region has its own unique concerns about weather, natural disasters and geological features, every community center would have to be designed to best utilize energy resources while planning for potential disasters. One way to achieve this goal is by holding an international architecture contest, inviting people from all over the world to submit their designs and the reasons behind them. Local architecture, construction, green energy and emergency professionals could examine the submissions and choose the three that best meet the center's needs. Ideally, an award would be given to the top three, regardless of whether or not the full designs were actually utilized.

Homeless Shelter

The community center will include a homeless shelter that is specifically designed to provide emergency housing to as many people as possible. However, this shelter would be operated by a non-profit organization with the appropriate knowledge and experience.

Capsule Design Sleeping Area

Based on the Japanese Capsule Hotel a shelter could be designed to hold a significantly larger number of able-bodied adults in the same amount of space. Capsules are about the size and shape of a coffin, so there is enough room for a single person and a limited number of personal belongings. The hotels build them into the wall, along with small step ladders that provide access to the upper capsules.

One of the advantages of the capsule design is the small glass door on each capsule, providing both privacy and security to the persons staying at the shelter. These doors could be designed to lock (or latch) from the inside, while remaining accessible to shelter staff with the appropriate key. This could help to reduce conflicts between people staying at the shelter, by reducing the opportunity for theft and physical attack while a person is sleeping. It also protects the people in the lower capsules from any property, linens or bodily fluids that might otherwise fall from the upper bunk. In addition, the shelter as a whole and the capsules specifically could be designed for regular power washing. This would make cleaning the facilities easier for shelter staff and volunteers.

Chronic Addiction Related Homelessness

This physical design would allow the homeless shelter in the community center to specifically address able-bodied adults who have been dealing with chronic homelessness as a direct result of issues with addiction. Once built, the shelter could send word out to all area non-profits that a large amount space was now available to house this very specific segment of the homeless population – allowing other shelters and organizations to recommend people to the new shelter.

Ideally, word would get around and people who habitually sleep in abandoned buildings, alleys, broken down cars, cardboard boxes, sewer lines and other hobbled-together shelters would begin to make a habit of using the targeted community center instead.

Disabilities and Families

On the down side, the capsules are not suitable for people with disabilities or families. Therefore, the shelter would be designed to hold as many able-bodied adults as possible, while working with existing shelters to help coordinate the re-allocation of existing resources. In this way, the new shelter would help to reduce the sheer number of people in need of emergency housing while allowing other shelters to focus on providing assistance to families and persons with disabilities.

Housing

The emphasis on 12-step programs, homeless shelters and soup kitchens makes this facility an excellent location for housing targeted to individuals who are unable to pass the background check required by most landlords. Therefore, a portion of the building would consist of small, utilitarian apartments managed by a non-profit organization committed to providing housing to recently released criminals and people with criminal records.

Jobs and Newspapers

Incorporating a non-profit that provides a work-related income stream to homeless people is an excellent way to help residents of the homeless shelter get off the street. Programs like Real Change, the homeless newspaper that provides people with an alternative to pan-handling are a perfect fit for this type of targeted community center.

However, it may be determined that for-profit organizations, such as Labor Ready, are equally beneficial to the people who utilize the community center. If that business is interested in renting space, then the non-profit managing the building may choose to rent space to that organization in the same way that space would be rented to for-profit bus lines.

Mail Service

This feature would be directly connected to the shelter, although it may be run by another non-profit. It also may be done in conjunction with a low-cost post office box service available to anyone.

Mail would be delivered to shelter residents through this non-profit. P.O. Box numbers would be assigned to each individual. Staff members would personally access and hand over mail when a shelter resident asks for it. In this way, residents can receive mail from any government agency, non-profit organization, potential employer, friends and family.

Parking Garage

The combination of a parking garage and a bus hub will make the facility fully accessible to everyone, including substance abuse treatment centers that regularly drop off van-loads of clients at 12-step meetings several times a week. This will also make it easier for area churches and other non-profits to provide free rides to a wide variety of resources, including church services, community events, medical care, job interviews and other targeted services.

Photo Identification

This office would be devoted entirely to helping people secure the necessary paperwork for a photo ID. Ideally, the creation of the identification would be completed on-site, but it may be necessary to simply help individuals find transportation to the appropriate government offices, once the necessary paperwork has been secured.

Public Library

This may seem like an odd addition to a targeted community center, but libraries are one of the most common places homeless people go when they need to kill time during the day or when the weather gets bad. There are a few reasons for this: 1) libraries are open to anyone, 2) books and computers are excellent ways to kill a few hours (even without a library card), 3) the buildings provide ample protection from the elements, 4) libraries tend to be open when homeless shelters are closed, and 5) free Wi-Fi and computer access allows everyone, regardless of financial situation, access to the internet.

The library already has the knowledge, skill and resources available to create and manage a free computer lab and building-wide Wi-Fi internet access. The community center provides a unique opportunity to provide the target population with access to technology as well as a wide range of books, magazines and newspapers -- including those specifically focused on addiction, homelessness and other issues of interest to this community of people.

It is extremely important that the community center and all participating non-profits avoid directly associating with or promoting a specific 12-step group. The public library has the unique ability to remain neutral while providing free access to books, magazine, workbooks and other materials produced by a wide range of 12-step programs.

If any of the non-profits providing services to children and youths wish to make a Red Bookshelf available to their clients, the public library may be able to assist in securing age-appropriate books. Also, there may be opportunities for hosting library programs in the youth-only and family-only areas.

Secure Storage

This feature would be directly connected to the shelter, although it may be run by another non-profit. Simply put, it is a short-term storage area. Individuals using the shelter would check in their extra belongings before going to bed at night, and then pick them up again in the morning.

The services provided could consist of anything from the storage boxes bus stations used to have (e.g.: plug in a quarter and pull out the key) to a large storage area manned by non-profit staff that provide a shelter resident with a 'coat-check number' when the belongings are placed on a shelf in a large and securely locked storage room.

Soup Kitchen

The community center will rent the kitchen and two eating areas to a non-profit skilled in managing a soup kitchen. One eating area would be geared toward adults and the other would be restricted to children and families. Ideally, this kitchen will provide at least three meals a day, seven days a week, as well as snacks and bag lunches to the youth-only area.

Children and Families

The eating area for children and families would have high chairs and other necessary supplies. It might collaborate with organizations that provide after school programs or fun activities for the children and youths who use various services on their own, through the youth-only area, or in conjunction with family members.

General Public

The general eating area is only loosely considered adults-only. The children and families area is provided for the protection of the children. However, there are times when families will choose to eat in the area open to the general public.

Pay What You Can

Because the building would be designed for the purpose of housing a soup kitchen, homeless shelter and other services; secure donation boxes could be built into the walls of the eating areas. This would allow people to discreetly pay whatever they can for their meal.

Encouraging Community Fellowship

It is a common practice among members of 12-step programs to 'fellowship' before and/or after a meeting. Encouraging people to utilize the soup kitchen and other areas of the community center for these casual social events increases the possibility that residents of the homeless shelter will interact with people who are involved in recovery. Also, it allows people who are financially better off the opportunity to support the soup kitchen while socializing with people who are less financially fortunate and unable to pay as much (or anything at all) toward a meal.

This same benefit could be equally useful to religious and non-profit organizations that volunteer their time or provide services to people utilizing the community center.

Youth-Only Area

The youth-only area would be designed for use by a non-profit organization focused on trying to help kids get off the street. The physical location in, or next to, the bus station provides ample opportunity to catch kids who are traveling across country, beginning the process of running away, or otherwise in danger of being preyed upon. Hopefully, they would be able to help these kids before the predators get to them, but many cases will involve helping these kids escape extremely dangerous and abusive situations.

24-Hour Access to Food

Providing the youth-only area in conjunction with a soup-kitchen and homeless shelter effectively brings together everything the kids are looking for when they are on the streets. These are the exact same things many predators use when luring a child away. This gives the non-profit managing the youth-only area direct access to additional and powerful resources.

Bus Lines

This feature of the targeted community center also provides a unique benefit to local and nation bus lines, which would be able to direct any and all children or youths traveling alone, for any reason, to spend their time in the youth-only area. Regardless of whether the child is a run-away, a street kid, or just a young person traveling across country alone, the youth-only area is a safe place to get help, find a meal or snack, or safely wait for the next bus or a family member to arrive.

Housing

The community center may choose to design he youth-only area to include housing for youths without families. Depending on the area, there may be a great need for safe emergency housing. Then again, there may be a well-established network of options already in place, which the employees of the youth-only area would plug into, without managing a youth-only homeless shelter. This is something that would have to be examined and addressed during the design of the building.

Chapter 4: Low Budget Lifestyles

There are precious few options for simple, low-budget living available. We need to increase the opportunities for cost-effective living in every region of this country while working to make the cost of housing more universally affordable. In most cases, truly low-budget housing would be available for no more than 25% of the current federal minimum wage, all utilities included. Basing the controlled rent price on the current federal minimum wage ensures that the cost truly is affordable for everyone. By creating a large number of housing options that fall within a truly affordable range and making them available to anyone, regardless of income level or credit rating, it may improve the overall quality and reliability of low-cost housing. Here are a few unique suggestions for housing developments that may help to meet the need for low budget housing options:

Anti-Luxury Housing

A new form of low-income housing, these utilitarian apartments would be built to last and available for rent at no more than 25% of the current minimum wage, all utilities included. Imagine a small efficiency apartment built to withstand a good power wash every year. The bathroom and kitchen have everything necessary – and nothing more. The front room may have a flat raised area the size of a queen size mattress and the kitchen could have a table and chairs built into the wall. There may even be picture hooks already embedded into the wall.

The inherent danger that comes with investing in this sort of development is universal rent increases. If the anti-luxury apartments are not kept within a carefully monitored system of rent control, there would be landlords who try to charge tenets the same price existing 'luxury' apartments are receiving. If successful, those 'luxury' apartments will significantly increase in price as well.

Disaster Prevention Low-Income Developments

In areas where natural disasters have struck multiple times, destroying mobile homes, houses and farms, it may prove cost effective to build a range of low-income housing designed to prevent this sort of destruction. Some apartments would fall under the 25% of minimum wage rule, while others would consist of homes that fall within the size and price range of an average mobile home. This housing would then be made available to everyone, particularly people currently living in exceptionally dangerous housing, such as mobile homes in tornado country.

For example, if a mobile home park located in an area known for tornados were moved entirely underground, residents would simply remain safely inside their homes until the storm passed. It may be possible to create an underground road that runs right through the community, allowing residents to drive in and out of their garages, just like they were living above ground. Or, it may make more sense to build the garages above ground, with direct access to the homes from inside the garages. Either way, the loss of a handful of garages or other utility buildings presents far less danger and a significantly lower cost than the complete destruction of an equal number of homes.

Parking Garage Apartments

The cost of these garage apartments would vary greatly from one region to the next, but the objective would be to keep them close to 25% of minimum wage, particularly in college towns and areas with a regular and significant change in the local population on an annual or seasonal basis.

Imagine a parking garage made entirely of private garages with locking gates. Each garage would be large enough to hold a reasonably large travel trailer or class C motor home and a standard sized car or truck. There would be hookups for electricity, water and sewage, as well as a minimal amount of storage space for regularly accessed items, such as bikes or surfboards. The garage would have temperature control but it would remain just above freezing and just below unbearably hot. The ground floor would have a rental office with PO office boxes for every resident, as well as a small convenience store.

Every garage would be rented out on a monthly basis, all utilities included. The target market would consist of college students, long distance commuters, people who work jobs that frequently change location and people who regularly leave the country for long periods of time.

During long absences, a tenant can choose to reduce the monthly cost by placing the vehicle and trailer in smaller storage areas located elsewhere in the garage, thereby reducing the hassle and cost that comes with trying to rent out a current apartment, get rid of furniture, place property in storage – or the opposite, when returning to the country.

The company managing the garage apartments might require every tenant to remove all property once or twice a year, in preparation for a scheduled power-washing, pest control treatment, and general inspection.

Small Business Condo-Malls

Imagine a multi-story mall filled with small and family businesses. The public area looks like any other mall, but behind the stores are private residences where the owners of the shops live. The combination would be geared toward creating an affordable option for small business owners, particularly those located in crowded urban areas.

These outward facing condos would have another, resident-only, walkway, allowing residents to stroll around the building and chat with neighbors without entering the mall. The developers may choose to create long windowed greenhouses along the outside of the building, providing residents with a uniquely urban 'yard' or garden space.

Tiny House Communities

Similar to standard trailer parks or housing developments, these communities would be designed to provide a small lot of land and all of the necessary electrical and water hook ups for tiny houses. In some cases, the land might be prepared for a tiny house in the same way that it would be prepared for a prefabricated home, and then sold to people who are looking for a permanent place to build or park their tiny home.

This could be particularly beneficial to areas with large numbers of houses sitting empty and falling into disrepair. Remove the existing houses, clear out and repartition the land. Take advantage of the opportunity to identify, fix and improve all aspects of the local infrastructure. Consider installing every lot with a backup generator hooked up to the electrical grid and the street light located closest to the lot. Potential buyers would be purchasing land, potentially reduced electrical costs, an off-grid power source, and the security that comes from a consistently operating street lamp.

Prepare the lots for use by a range of development options, including tiny houses, mobile homes, prefabricated homes, RV parking or storage, and standard construction. In this way, the yards can be increased and potential homeowners would be able to build, purchase, or park a small building that can be increased in size through future construction. Some people will choose to live in small low budget housing while taking full advantage of a large yard. Others will use the space to increase their home size, slowly, over time.

Of course, local government agencies would be best serviced by anticipating the possibility of regular home improvement and construction projects occurring in this area over the next few decades.

Chapter 5: Updating Education

There are five key points that must be covered in any discussion about education:

1) Identify the primary objective behind a public education
2) Establish a low baseline around the primary objectives
3) Provide flexibility for modification based on parental involvement
4) Create a schedule and a system suited to modern day work habits
5) Social skills, relationship building and school-time behavior expectations should be based on the realities of the modern workplace

Purpose of Public Education

Every program and organization must have a clear and achievable purpose that defines, in the simplest terms, the primary objectives. When it comes to public education, there are as many opinions about what it should be as there are people participating in the system. What I would like to propose is not what an education *should* be, but what it *must* be. After identifying those things that every student *must* know upon graduating a specific grade level, a realistic system, flexible enough to meet a wide range of unique needs and objectives, can be built.

One of the indicators of the relative success or failure of a school system is achievement scores on standardized tests, and how those scores compare to other countries. This is an unrealistic and meaningless competition. A more realistic approach would be to compare the school system to the United States Olympic Team:

> In 2012 there were millions of people participating in organized high school and college athletics, but only 530 athletes attended the summer Olympic Games in London, England. Comparatively speaking, expecting our students to achieve universally high test scores is like expecting every athlete in the country to qualify for the Olympic Games.

When it comes right down to it, some people have the talent and the drive to achieve greatness (in any form) and other people do not. The school system should not be expected to produce millions of mathematical geniuses like some kind of humanoid computer factory. A school is not successful only when students achieve high test scores any more than a community athletics program is only successful when participating athletes compete on an international level. These are good and admirable achievements, but they are unrealistic expectations.

The services a public school provides to a community can be best broken down as follows:

1. Teaching students the skills and knowledge necessary for employment.
2. Teaching students what they need to know about government, laws and the responsibilities of citizenship.
3. Addressing the unique needs and concerns of both the students and the families utilizing the schools system.
4. Provide opportunities for advanced learning and skill building.

Ultimately, the quality of a school can be best measured by the level of satisfaction expressed by the people utilizing the services it provides.

Definition of Success

Some people will spend their entire lives working a blue-collar or service job, and that's OK! It is possible to carve out a very good life by remaining focused on raising a family or living a simple and quiet life without pursuing an advanced degree or anything more than a job that pays the bills. A public school education should provide the knowledge and skills necessary to achieve that kind of life.

Conversely, it is not the responsibility of the school system to identify an individual's passion or calling in life. The way these things are fostered and developed is through personal ambition and achievement. For example, if a student completes a GED and the technical training necessary for working as an auto mechanic, and later discovers that he or she hates spending everyday on the inside of an engine, the school system was still successful in achieving its primary objectives. That auto mechanic can take those skills and find a job that pays well enough to cover the bills, pursue an advanced education, or watch for opportunities to move into a different position within the automotive industry.

Four-Year Classes

An educational system based on the needs of an agricultural (seasonal) society no longer meets the needs of most families and employers. Students need to learn to work with a teacher in the same manner that an employee works with a manager. This means developing long-term relationships, establishing firm grounds for mutual respect, and adhering to a year-round class schedule.

One way to achieve these goals is through small four-year classes. Under this system, a group of 25 (or less) students would work year-round with the same teacher for four years. During that time, students would study everything needed to pass one of three general education exams.

Classroom Objectives and Time Management

Every teacher spends a significant amount of time during the first month of school simply establishing discipline, getting to know the students and evaluating where each student falls academically. By allowing a teacher to work with the same kids for an entire four year period that process will only have to occur one time. Also, this significantly reduces the possibility of sending a student into the next grade, just to avoid dealing with a problem.

Grades 1-4

It is physically unnatural for a human being to spend enormous amounts of time bent over a desk. It is even more unnatural for a child to spend an entire day sitting down, much less bent over a pile of worksheets. Because the teacher works with these students year-round, it is reasonable to expect the children to spend half of their day playing outside, going on fieldtrips or participating in physically active learning games.

Grades 5-8

Gradually, more time is spent sitting at a desk, but students are still provided with regular opportunities for exercise and hands-on experiences. Emphasis moves away from simply exploring the world as students are provided opportunities for job shadowing, volunteering, conducting research and preparing for the 8th grade general education exam.

Grades 9-12

Initial focus in on passing the standard GED exam and students spend full workdays preparing. Once a student has passed the GED, the assigned teacher will work with him or her to identify the technical training that is best suited to the student's skills set, academic strengths and long-term objectives.

When technical school begins, the student will attend classes in the traditional style, moving between his or her main classroom and the courses offered in other areas of the school or in other schools entirely. At this point, the teacher operates as a mentor, tutor, and manager, helping the student to maintain a realistic schedule and meet all assigned goals and deadlines.

When a student passes the GED, it is his or her choice to either take advantage of a free technical education or to officially 'graduate' and end their academic involvement. Every student who chooses to pursue a technical degree or certification will graduate with a clearly documented set of marketable skills.

Discipline and Relationships

Each teacher would be able to establish discipline and build meaningful relationships with every student in his or her classroom. In turn, students will also develop relationships with the teacher and with each other, learning about social skills and acceptable academic or professional behavior.

Respect is something that is earned. Establishing a healthy long-term relationship is one of the most effective ways to earn another person's respect. By providing teachers the opportunity to form these relationship[s, students would have the ability to develop trust, admiration and respect for an authority figure. Also, they will develop strong relationships with each other and, hopefully, over time those relationships would be founded in mutual respect.

Small Classrooms

Keeping the classes to a reasonably small size of no more than 25 students' increases a teacher's ability to identify and address the unique needs of each and every student. It also allows ample opportunity to provide one-on-one attention whenever and wherever necessary.

Students Set The Pace

Teachers will get to know the unique needs, strengths, weaknesses and ambitions of each and every student. The extended amount of time provided for working with a particular group will allow him or her to address specific needs or concerns one-on-one, almost like a tutoring session, without having to worry about taking valuable time and attention away from the other students.

Because the primary objective is to pass the general education exam, the classroom content would be tailored to meet that objective. However, the exam is a pass-fail test with the option to retake as many times as necessary and a student can take the test at any point during the four years spent under this teacher. Therefore, a student who is academically advanced may take and pass the exam much earlier than his or her classmates. Or, a student who is exceptionally good at math, may proceed through all the information required for the test much faster than the rest of the class, allowing the teacher to challenge that student with more advanced math lessons, while working with him or her on the topics that come more slowly.

In short, as long as all of the basic information required in the standardized test is covered during the four-years allocated, the teacher can move as quickly, or as slowly, as the students need.

Two-Week Vacation

Both students and teachers can take a two-week vacation, at any time of year, without fear of negative consequences. This is particularly helpful to families who need to attend a family function (e.g.: weddings, family reunions, anniversaries, etc.) during traditional school months. Because a teacher works with the same students for an extended period of time, it is reasonable to expect the student to take a two week vacation without fear of falling behind. Also, this will create a classroom culture that is more in line with the realities of the modern workplace.

Year-Round Classes

Keeping students involved year round creates a reliable schedule that is beneficial to both the students and the parents. Parents will not have to worry about paying for childcare three months out of the year and students will not have readjust to the school schedule every fall. In neighborhoods where children and youths with too much unsupervised idle time is a frequent cause for concern, this will provide a much-needed source of activities, guidance and structure.

Parental Involvement

Parents need more opportunities to participate in all aspects of the educational system. Schools systems need to become more focused on identifying and addressing both the needs of students and the expectations of parents. By setting the standardized educational requirements as low as possible, this provides each school the flexibility needed to develop and manage individualized classrooms, based on the decisions made by the parents involved.

Encourage Parental Collaboration

When groups of like-minded parents join together to make decisions about content and participate in the selection of a teacher, everyone benefits. Instead of simply assigning random students to a class, create an application system that allows parents to choose to work together. In this way, the school system would be able to cut down on tensions caused by parents with opposing opinions about everything from acceptable content to allowable methods of discipline. Also, it would be natural for people with similar priorities and objectives to develop a cohesive group. For example, a collection of 25 families who are strong supporters of the arts will seek out a teacher who can develop a curriculum that is very different from a collection of families who are primarily concerned about the sciences or college preparation.

Taken from another angle, the school system could also provide a list of potential teachers with a thorough description of their background, training, experience, academic strengths, and any relevant hobbies. Parents could then choose the teacher they are most interested in and provide a list of reasons why. From there, the school system could begin to form potential classrooms based on the mutual interests, objectives and concerns expressed by the parents.

Hiring Teachers

When a classroom is being formed, the parents would be given the opportunity to participate in identifying key issues in the areas of content and scheduling, crafting a job description, and interviewing potential teachers. School administrators would consult with parents at every step in the process, seriously considering individual feedback as well as group decisions.

Preregistration

Allow parents to request a spot in a specific teacher's classroom during the third year. In this way, parents who have come to know the teacher and his or her work through friends and family can request a spot in that classroom in advance. In many cases, this will simplify both the hiring process and the classroom expectations because most parents will just ask for the same thing that was provided to previous students.

By the same token, parents who are unsure about existing teachers or classrooms, should be provided the ability to list the qualities they are looking for, as well as any concerns they may have, during a pre-registration process beginning at least one-year before class start.

Content Decisions

There are two categories of decisions that must be addressed: 1) controversial issues and 2) parental expectations.

Controversial issues include things like evolution vs. intelligent design, specific perspectives on historic events, or the inclusion of sex education. When parents object to the presentation of information that will appear on the standardized test, the school system administrator would have to make it clear that it is necessary to cover the information in a manner that will allow the students to pass the exam, but alternative information can also be presented. For example, if evolution is a hot-button issue, the teacher can repeatedly remind students that the information may appear on the exam, and the correct answers will consist of the following information. That class work can be further tempered with information on intelligent design, which would be unique to this specific classroom.

Parental expectations are topics and objectives outside of the requirements of the standardized test. This could include anything from regularly planned art projects to immersion in a foreign language. In some cases it would be based entirely on what the parents consider to be important in a child's education. In other cases it would be a matter of addressing the unique needs of a community of families whose primary language is not English or who happen to share a common culture or skill, such as sign language. As long as the students are fully prepared for the standardized test, the teacher can fully utilize the remaining time to cover a wide range of parental expectations.

Flexible Scheduling

When a new classroom is being formed, the school will survey the scheduling limitations of all parents. Standard school hours may be modified to meet the needs of the families involved, particularly if the parents specifically request this change. Potentially, a classroom could be scheduled to begin much earlier or later than usual. This would make it much easier for parents working second and third shifts to coordinate the family schedule and to take advantage of opportunities to participate in school events. When a classroom is being established, unusual time schedules would be clearly detailed in the job description.

Identifying a Good Fit

Ultimately, the administrators make the hiring decision, but the objective is to find a good fit for each four-year classroom. The teacher needs to be able to communicate effectively with both the parents and the students. Because the job requires working very closely with a small group of students and their parents for an extended period of time, it is extremely important that the teacher is fully suited to all aspects of the job.

Reviewing Performance

Regular performance reviews would be conducted by school administrators, in conjunction with both parents and students. While student reviews would become more significant in grades five and higher, parental reviews will remain consistently important throughout. Whenever possible, schools will meet with parents and conduct surveys about their concerns and their overall level of satisfaction. As long as the parents are reasonably satisfied and the students are on track to pass the standardized test, the teacher will receive a positive review.

Standardized Tests

Based on the existing GED exam, all standardized tests would be written to test the minimal amount of knowledge required of a student at each of three points in his or her education. The knowledge bar is set as low as possible, allowing teachers and students the ability to achieve the national expectations without having to sacrifice spending time and resources on other topics and objectives. To this end, every student in the country would take the same exam and every teacher would be provided with a detailed description of the topics, potential questions and expected answers.

A student can choose to take the test at any point and there is no limit to the number of times a student can retake the exam. These are pass/fail exams. Only the current status of the exam is recorded – no numeric score or record of the number of retakes.

Technical School Guaranteed

Like it or not, a high school diploma is practically worthless. It's significantly better than no diploma or GED, but it doesn't mean much too potential employers. While technical school training does not guarantee employment, it significantly improves the value of a high school education because it provides students with a set of concrete and marketable skills. Also, students who are disillusioned about the value of a high school education may be more inclined to graduate when it is combined with technical school training.

Open To All Ages

The same features and benefits should be provided to all students, regardless of age. If necessary, the school system should create special classes filled with young people who are significantly older than the rest of the students in that grade level, students who are dealing with similar life issues (e.g.: pregnancy, homelessness, abuse, addiction, criminal records), or adults who are returning to complete a high school education.

Reducing Duplicate Services

Many school systems maintain complete on-site libraries, as well as facilities and supplies for athletics, art, and music programs or events. These are all very positive aspects to the educational experience. They are also services that are provided by other organizations, resulting in unnecessary duplication of resources.

A potential money-saving option for communities struggling to deal with budgets issues among area schools, as well as local government and non-profit organizations, is to eliminate some of the overlap.

Libraries

Hand responsibility and control of school libraries over to the public library system. Students can use a public library card at school and utilize all online services. Books can be reserved through the public library website and delivered to the school. Funding reserved for school system libraries can be provided to the public library in exchange for the management of school library needs.

Parks and Recreation

City park and recreation departments often maintain athletic facilities of all kinds. They also regularly manage a wide variety of sporting events and sports teams, along with opportunities to participate in the arts. If a school were to hand over all athletic fields, swimming pools, theaters and other similar resources to the park and recreation department, it would increase the opportunities available to the community as a whole while reducing the school's expenses.

Also, students would continue to have ample opportunity to participate, outside of classroom hours, in all of the sporting and artistic events previously managed by the school. Students would not be able to receive preferential treatment on days when a big game or competition was being held, but would be able to continue playing, regardless of any problems they may be having at school.

This would be most useful in communities where the parks and recreation and department is actively expanding its offering and services while area schools are struggling with cutbacks and securing the funding needed to stay open without laying off teachers.

Chapter 6: Scholarship Competitions

An increase in competitive events resulting in full-ride scholarships would he extremely helpful to a large number of people currently trying to pay for a college education or other advanced training.

Universal Opportunity

Students who have not received a quality education (for any number of reasons) are at an immediate disadvantage when trying to secure funding for college. Scholarships and academic awards are frequently based on advanced academic achievement or exceptional athletic ability. Even students who have managed to achieve one of those things, despite the challenges present in their lives, may not be selected to receive one of the few full-ride scholarships available.

Creating competitions that provide a large number of full-ride scholarships to every student who successfully competes, helps to address the failings present in our current educational system. It also allows both schools and potential employers to briefly meet students who are proving their determination to better themselves by simply showing up.

Intelligent vs. Educated

Most people make the mistake of assuming someone who is uneducated is also lacking in intelligence. While this is a glaringly obvious falsehood, the fact remains that people who are both intelligent and uneducated are not provided the opportunities needed to obtain an education or otherwise succeed in life. A competition open to anyone who chooses to participate would help to provide those sorely needed opportunities. Designing the competition to test resourcefulness, persistence, and problem solving, instead of a specific body of knowledge, will help to separate out those people who are lacking only in a formal education.

College Entry Guaranteed

People who manage to prove their potential by earning a competitive scholarship are guaranteed entry into a college or university, but they are not, necessarily, academically prepared for college level classes.

Winners would be provided with the tutoring they need to bring their knowledge and academic skills up to college level. Tutoring would then continue for as long as the students needs.

In addition to academic tutoring, these students would also receive training, coaching or other assistance in the areas of communication, office politics and acceptable workplace behavior. By making preparations for the expectations of the workplace an integral part of the student's college experience, the odds of success are significantly increased in the student's favor.

In short, if an individual is determined enough to get into college by plowing through one of these competitions, then they deserve the opportunity to earn an advanced degree.

Testing Potential Employees

In addition to testing the mettle of potential students, the competition would provide an excellent opportunity to evaluate the personality and talent of a potential employee. In fact, some competitors may choose to participate in an effort to impress recruiters from various companies or branches of the military.

In many ways, this is very similar to the recruitment efforts that occur during international computer hacking competitions or conferences that offer individuals the opportunity to show off their work, skills, and knowledge. The primary difference is the target audience – people who have not had the opportunity to access the resources that would provide them those kinds of specialized skills, and people whose talents and skill set fall could be described as broad-based trouble-shooting, resourcefulness and sheer determination.

Example Competition

Several universities and colleges struggling to find an effective way of dealing with chronic and potentially fatal hazing traditions, join forces with all branches of the military, a few sporting equipment companies, an extreme challenge event planning company, MTV and other members of the media whose primary focus is the young adult and college student market.

Objective: Reduce Hazing

The competition has three objectives: 1) create an event that tests and challenges participants in such a way that it trumps all known hazing methods, 2) directly affect the fabric of hazing-effected student organizations by partially controlling the people involved, and 3) support the schools involved by providing a large number of determined students with full-ride scholarships.

Student Organizations

Each school would approach the organizations dealing with chronic hazing problems or recent incidents involving the hospitalization or injury of students. After discussing the gravity of the situation, school rules, and the options available, these organizations will either agree to remove itself from the campus and all aspects of university life, or automatically award membership to any interested student holding a competition-provided scholarship.

The student organizations would be made well aware of the amount of national press this event will receive. Also, the competition itself would be widely advertised in terms that challenge the concept of hazing, such as: anyone can drink, let's see what you've really got.

The Winners

Every student who enters the competition is eligible to win a full-ride scholarship. If 3000 scholarships are available, then 3000 slots would be open to students interested in competing. The objective is to complete the challenge presented. There is no need to try and eliminate competitors and, depending on the nature of the event, it may be beneficial for participants to join together and work as a team.

The Scholarship and Other Prizes

The scholarship is a full-ride, four-year scholarship available to students pursuing both undergraduate and graduate degrees. In addition, the event planners may choose to have custom designed jewelry or tattoos available only to people who successfully complete the challenge.

Preliminary Recruitment and Advertising

Preliminary recruiting, advertising and media events must make it clear that the colleges and universities involved do not receive funding until the winners enroll. Unused scholarships are returned to the individuals and organizations donating the funds. This initial recruitment campaign may place a portion of the spotlight on the impressive bragging rights that come with successfully completing the challenge, as well as the winners-only jewelry and tattoos.

Pre-Challenge Preparation

Offer a free boot camp to all aspiring competitors or to all accepted competitors. This could be used as a preliminary competition, narrowing down the field to the total number of slots available, or it could be strictly focused on providing the training necessary to successfully and safely complete the event. Either way, competitors only need to show up. Once there, everything would be provided for them – food, clothes, housing and a thorough training program.

This is an excellent opportunity for event planners to identify the various individual challenges participants are facing. This will help schools to plan for the arrangement of tutors focused on addressing everything from academic knowledge to professional behavior.

Collection of representatives from participating media and public relations professionals will utilize a portion of this time to provide specialized training in the best way to speak to an interviewer, behave on camera, and handle the media both during and after the competition.

Reality Television

While there would be a reality-television element to the event, it would be best approached in the same manner as the Olympics. Interviewers will do biographical research on all competitors and run short interviews with the individuals, family and friends. While the focus will naturally fall on those competitors who finish first, the best possible ending will involve every competitor successfully finishing the challenge.

The Challenge

The most difficult aspect to this event would be creating something that truly tests the resourcefulness, problem-solving capabilities and determination of the participants without placing too much emphasis on standard academics or physical stamina. Also, it is important that proper security measures are taken, to prevent serious injuries or accidents.

The challenge itself could be as simple as a specially designed week-long triathlon or a 25 mile hike through rough wilderness with nothing but a map, compass and backpack full of supplies. It could consist of a series of challenges and puzzles ranging from the primarily physical to the purely intellectual problem-solving.

Ultimately, it is up to the universities and all participating organizations to develop and approve all aspects of the challenge and ensure that the competitors are provided every opportunity to receive the training necessary to succeed. Regardless of the specific details, the end result must consist of something the average American college student would find both highly impressive and extremely difficult.

Chapter 7: An American Dream for the Future

A safety net most effective when it is combined with a long-term plan geared toward significantly reducing the need for assistance. Simply informing the public that benefits and services will cease to exist on a specific date reduces the amount of money paid into the system, but it does nothing to reduce the *need* for those services. Creating an economy that is truly solid and self-reliant requires both a vibrant network of small-businesses and a widespread change in our definition of the 'American Dream.'

Ultimately, it is up to every individual to identify a personal interpretation of the 'American Dream' and pursue it to the best of his or her ability but, individuals, entrepreneurs and communities all over the country are best served by working to create a private economy with minimal reliance on government assistance. There will always be taxes, laws and regulations. By reducing the need for government involvement, the new political, social and economic environment may help to naturally reduce the overall size of government, as well as the level of government involvement in our professional and private lives.

The Reality of Need

Even if all of the following suggestions (and more) became commonplace, there would still be a need for human services programs like those described in this book, as well as those currently in existence. Unfortunately, sometimes unanticipated catastrophes occur, despite the best of planning. Also, there will always be individuals who do not follow the best given advice, and people who are unfairly victimized by the poor choices of others.

While it is in everyone's best interest to work toward a standard of life and an economic culture that significantly reduces the overall need and habitual reliance on government programs, it must never be assumed that the need will one day disappear.

Need vs. Want

Identifying the difference between need and want has two primary parts: 1) reducing expenses by setting priorities based on true need and 2) significantly changing the standard lifestyle to reduce the total number of things that are necessary.

Necessities

Recognizing that the average family true needs only a small fraction of the many thousands of things available for purchase is a small but important step. High school home economics classes are traditionally focused on the skills necessary to complete the duties of a traditional housewife. The same class could be modified to teach both teenagers and adults the difference between things that are necessary for survival, things that are necessary for employment, and things that are essentially luxuries. A significant portion of the American population can neither bake a loaf of bread from scratch nor create a true list of necessities.

Regaining the ability to separate need from want is an essential step in the path to self sufficiency. Creating and managing small businesses will generate cash flow, but that cash must be properly managed with an eye toward long-term sustainability. Therefore, business owners must be able to spend wisely in both their professional and private lives.

Changing Reality

Reducing the number of cars of the road would provide a long list of environmental, structural, social, and security benefits. Some people have suggested that the price of gas or vehicles should be artificially inflated, forcing people to cease using private transportation. Others have tried to push through laws forbidding the purchase of a vehicle. None of these options will work because these do not address the core reality – vehicles have become a necessity that outweighs our relative desire to own (or not own) one.

Our current reality requires the use of a vehicle to get to work, school, after school functions, family events, worship services, the grocery store, and hundreds of other necessary aspects of our lives. While some people own vehicles for pleasure, all people own vehicles out of necessity.

If it were possible to keep your job but eliminate your daily commute, would you do it? If it were possible to safely send your kids on a short walk to school every day, instead of dropping them off or waiting for the bus, would you take advantage of the option? If it were possible to eliminate the need for a vehicle entirely, would your life become significantly less stressful?

A large number of people in this country would answer all of these questions with an emphatic 'Yes!' Currently, families in many regions of the United States find it extremely difficult to manage without at least one reliable vehicle, even when an adequate public transit system is available. Yet, most people would prefer to eliminate that need, and that expense, from their lives.

One way to achieve this goal is to purchase a building that is zoned for both business and residential, move into the residential side and open a small business in the storefront. Another option is to put an office into your home and arrange to telecommute to your current job. Yet another option is to gather together a group of friends and family to discuss the establishment of an intentional community and several cooperative family businesses. In fact, there are as many different ways to achieve this goal as there are people interested in pursuing it. The key is to take a good hard look at your life, goals, and challenges, and determine which option is best for you.

Owning a vehicle is just one of many items that are a necessity because of our current cultural and economic realities. Change those realities and you change the list of necessities. One of the easiest ways to achieve this kind of change is by specifically identifying items that need to be modified or eliminates, and developing small businesses (or creating a lifestyle/work environment) designed to reduce or eliminate those specific items.

Going Green

Going green is an admirable and environmentally friendly way to go. It's also a good business decisions simply because many of the options available can significantly reduce the cost of utilities both immediately and over the long term. It makes good sense to seriously consider all of the green energy, energy efficiency, and green building material options when building, repairing, or moving into a new business or home.

In addition to cost savings, installing something as simple as a backup generator connected to the electrical grid can be an important security feature in the event of a brown-out, black-out, natural disaster or other emergency. If the generator runs on diesel and it is installed in a restaurant that serves fried food, then learning how to convert used vegetable oil into bio-diesel could greatly reduce the cost of running the generator.

Real Estate

There will always be a real estate market and the widespread existence of investment properties. Whether it's housing available for rent or commercially zoned property being bought, sold or utilized by companies of all sizes, the need will always exist.

The problem is not in the existence of the real estate market, but our cultural dependence upon that market as a pillar within our economy. Private homes, farms, protected wild lands and even the property utilized by small businesses should never be viewed as a financial investment. It is a key aspect to our ability to establish a community, raise a family, grow food, and pass our culture, history and traditions down through generations.

Everything associated with a real estate transaction or even the modification or improvement on an existing property, should be done with an eye toward the very distant future. When we, as a community and culture, modify our perception of both the use and value of real estate as a whole, we would be able to make decisions and take actions that protect and insulate ourselves and our families from the kind of wide-spread financial catastrophe that occurred in 2008.

Regulations within the financial sector were a necessary and important aspect to the enormous amount of work required to clean up that particular mess —but they are only half of the story. The consumers also played a part in the market crash. We must recognized, accept and work toward changing those lifestyle and cultural habits that helped to contribute to the problem, because that is the best possible way to protect ourselves from future predatory behavior, as well as the widespread fallout from the next financial disaster.

Not a Market Commodity

Investing in the home is for the purpose of addressing the needs of current and future generations. Decisions should never be based on 'market value.' It is a home, an heirloom and a physical structure that directly affects and supports the community of people living in and around it. Instead, focus on finding ways to improve both the property and the surrounding community, for the purpose of preserving and preparing for the next generation.

Want vs. Need

How much house does an individual or family really need? One of the advantages to buying a tiny house and building on it, slowly, over time, is that the building expands to meet the actual needs of the people living in it. Regardless of whether a family chooses to grow a tiny house or purchase an average sized home, it is important to identify just how much is truly necessary.

Community Focused

Housing development should be approached in a manner similar to wildlife preservation – identify the needs of the people who live there and provide the physical requirements necessary for meeting those needs across many generations. While building a neighborhood of similar-looking houses that end in a serious of cul-de-sacs and are located within walking distance of a school or a playground is a good beginning, it does not address the true core issue.

Developing community means bringing together people, establishing relationships, and finding ways to maintain those relationships over the long term. If a large family or other, similar, community of people got together and decided to create a housing development for themselves, their children and their grandchildren, then it may, or may not, look like a standard housing development. Even if the end result looked exactly like the kinds of housing developments found all over the country, there would be one key difference – the people living there and the widespread commitment to maintaining a claim on this section of land for many generations to come. In other words, the problem isn't in the architecture, it's in the attitude.

Breaking the Reliance on Big Business

There are hundreds of news stories published about factories and other large businesses which managed to avoid financial ruin by eliminating existing pensions. Current workers got to keep their jobs and retired workers lost their annual income. These are tragic cautionary tales about the danger in relying on an employer for your future financial security.

Businesses, both large and small, should never be viewed as benevolent caretakers. They are customers paying workers for specific services. By moving the control of key investments, like retirement accounts and health insurance, into the hands of employees, those workers gain a very powerful bargaining position. Simply put, if a person does not need a job to cover living expenses or benefits, then it becomes significantly harder for a company to force that employee to put up with low pay, unrealistic expectations, poor working conditions, or abusive behavior. Also, when the paycheck isn't necessary for survival, it is far easier to negotiate for a higher wage.

Community-Wide Financial Security

There are cities and towns all over the country that stand as monuments to the destruction caused by over reliance on big business. When the factories shut down, the primary employer closes shop, or a series of large corporations decide to send a significant portion of their workforce overseas, the community is drained of crucial financial resources. Before long, a formerly vibrant and active community can become little more than an empty shell filled with a few unemployed stragglers and a handful of small businesses on the verge of going under.

Factories and big business enhance an economy, they do not create it. A town that lives by this statement, and aggressively fosters small business development, regardless of how many (often low paying) jobs similar large companies may be offering, will survive the inevitable closure of those factories and office buildings. Communities that remain focused on the big numbers and the pretty headlines lavishing praise on corporations that create those promised jobs, will eventually find themselves looking at physical and financial ruin.

Factories, corporations, and big business of all kinds have one thing in common – they exist to make money. Many put forth an admirable effort to provide decent pay and good benefits for their employees and make donations of time, money and other resources to area non-profits and community organizations. But, when it comes down to it, the company will make decisions based on the bottom line, not on the needs of the community where it currently happens to reside.

Small businesses have significantly more invested in the overall quality and sustainability of the surrounding community. All aspects to the life and culture of a small business owner's hometown, directly affects his or her professional and private life.

Not only do local businesses have significantly more to lose, they become the pillars upon which the community relies after large corporations leave town. If the small business community is strong, vibrant and continually growing in size and variety, then the elimination of a factory or other big business will not completely destroy the town.

Political Incentive

Politicians tend to pursue good press. Being able to announce the creation of several hundred jobs due to negotiations with a large corporation, or as a direct result of tax breaks offered to manufacturing companies, makes very good press. Unfortunately, developing hundreds of small family businesses takes a significantly more time, resources and the risk of coming under fire in the media for not 'doing more.'

The Guaranteed Work Program (GWP) described in chapter one has a firm emphasis on helping people acquire the money needed to start a small business. Establishing a national program that provides jobs and resources for small business development to any American Citizen or legal resident provides an excellent opportunity for good press at the outset. It also provides additional opportunities for politicians to inform the press that multiple businesses have been successfully established as a direct result of aggressive small business development efforts – along with equally positive announcements about the number of local residents who have managed to break out of the cycle of poverty and reliance on government assistance by starting a family business.

Investing in a town's financial future extends beyond a couple hundred low paying jobs and the income generated from the upcoming holiday shopping season. A region would be on its way to an economy based on long-term financial reliability when politicians start spending less time announcing the anticipated opening of factories and more time announcing the number of small businesses recently established.

Homemade Safety Nets

The key to creating a truly effective network of homemade safety nets is to prepare for the future as though the government would be unable or unwilling to provide the necessary assistance. This may sound a bit extreme, but it is an important mind-set to cultivate when dealing with long-term financial plans and problems.

Think about it like this: if a time came when the government was barely capably of protecting our borders and preventing all-out-chaos in the form of violent riots nationwide, what would be your primary concerns? For most people, those concerns would consist of the safety of family, the safety of friends, protecting family-owned land, and finding the necessary resources for survival – more or less in that order.

Now think of a less exciting scenario, such as the completely elimination of all human services benefits including, social security, SNAP (formerly known as food stamps), health care, and subsidized housing. Even if you yourself were not relying on these things, chances are good you know someone whose survival depends on them. Also, the sudden massive increase of homeless people entering the shelters and the streets after losing access to low-income and subsidized housing would create potentially dangerous and mob-like environments all over the country. Consider the possibility and, once again, ask yourself: what are your primary concerns? Chances are very good they would be the same concerns as those listed in the previous scenario.

The bottom line is this: when faced with an emergency situation the average human being will place priority on the safety of family, friends and a specific geographic territory (e.g.: home). This is natural, instinctual, and crucial to our survival as a species. It's also the exact opposite of the way in which most Americans live their day-to-day lives.

While creating an effective homemade safety net does not require building a bunker and stockpiling weapons out in the wilderness somewhere, it does require a similar mindset when approaching all financial decisions. Ultimately, it comes down to this:

- Enjoy the joyful moments however they arrive
- Address the needs of today
- Prepare for the problems of tomorrow
- Plan for both the amazing successes and the devastating catastrophes of the distant future
- Trust there will always be joys and problems aplenty

Entrepreneurial Home Economics

Entrepreneurial home economics is a method of approaching the numbers behind both a family business and a family budget. If the accounting is properly managed, the business becomes the firm foundation holding up all other financial decisions and obligations a family might have. The objective is to manage the business so that it provides enough money, durable goods and benefits (e.g.: health insurance, life insurance, etc.) to meet all of the family's basic needs. If every member of the family with an outside job suddenly found themselves unemployed, the family business would continue to provide all of the financial support necessary. Things would be tight, but they would be workable.

For example: Jane Doe manages a small corner grocery store which pulls in enough money to cover her family's basic expenses, including deposits into the emergency fund, insurance and the full cost of health care. John Doe, her husband, does freelance design work from a home office and occasionally commutes to the local factory to complete longer-term contracts on-site. All of the money John earns goes into the retirement fund, vacation fund, entertainment fund, and emergency fund. When the factory closes, John simply focuses on freelance work and occasionally helps out in the grocery store.

Baby Businesses

It is common for a family budget to include a college savings fund. The assumption is that children will complete a college degree, find a good paying job and start the process all over again. This is a good plan and one that most people should continue utilizing within the standard family budget.

In fact, the family business should establish a similar fund, putting away a percentage of annual profits for the purpose of establishing additional businesses in the future. In most cases, the future business owners would be the children of the current business owner, but some people may choose to assist other family members, friends or reliable employees. Regardless of whom the recipient may be, the baby business fund is a nest egg for the establishment of additional small and family businesses within the community.

Backup Employment

One of the great advantages to small and family businesses is the availability of work for family members. Instead of simply supporting adult children (or other family members) who move back home after finishing college or losing a job, business owners and farmers have the ability to put those people to work. The pay may not be particularly large, but when it comes with housing, utilities, food and health care, it can be a lifesaver.

Emergency Housing

Creating an emergency housing resource within a family or close circle of friends requires not only the physical space, but the ability to establish clear and firm ground rules. No one likes to be taken advantage of and, frankly, people who are struggling with poverty or a temporary emergency situation do not like being labeled as lazy freeloaders.

Some families have already taken advantage of a unique real estate situation and turned it into a resource for the entire family. For example, when a relative dies and leaves a reasonably well maintained, and fully paid-for, property to someone who already has a home, then this newly empty house becomes a perfect place for family members who are in need of a low-cost place to live.

Other reasonable options might include:

1. A finished attic or basement.
2. A guest room in a house.

3. The rooms previously vacated by children who have moved out.

4. A refinished carriage house or mother-in-law apartment.

5. A newly constructed apartment attached to an existing home or built over a garage.

6. A finished area inside a barn or other farm building.

7. A private community center with emergency housing facilities, built by a collection of families or an intentional community.